THE GERMANS FROM RUSSIA IN OKLAHOMA

by Douglas Hale

D1714939

Oklahoma Image is a project sponsored by the
Oklahoma Department of Libraries
and the Oklahoma Library Association,
and made possible by a grant from the
National Endowment for the Humanities.

Library of Congress Cataloging in Publication Data

Hale, Douglas.
  The Germans from Russia in Oklahoma

  (Newcomers to a new land)
  Bibliography: p.
  1. Russian Germans in Oklahoma — History.   2. Oklahoma —
History.   I. Title.   II. Series.
F705.R85H34   976.6'004'31   79-20152

ISBN 978-0-8061-1620-4 (paper)

CONTENTS

For John Rath

PREFACE

This little book is about ordinary people who through a series of circumstances led extraordinary lives. For the most part, the Germans who came from Russia to Oklahoma were honest farmers who never courted fame or aspired to great power or influence. The majority were very poor when they settled here and remained in modest circumstances throughout their lives. There is little about them in the newspapers, and their origins were sufficiently obscure to confuse the census takers. Yet they were a remarkable people who embodied the real, as opposed to the mythical, qualities of the American pioneer. They had been pioneers before on the other side of the globe; they undertook the risky and uncertain adventure of immigration to America. And when they arrived, they did not hive off into enclaves of their own in the cities but sought to make their way in comparative isolation on the very edge of the frontier. Without knowledge of the land they were settling, the techniques of American agriculture, or even the language itself, they still came. This required more courage than most of us possess, more self-reliance, and more faith in the future.

Only within the last decade have the Germans from Russia found many new voices to express their character, recount their experiences, and celebrate their achievements. Other states—Nebraska, North and South Dakota, Kansas, Colorado, and California—have begun to recognize these people as a colorful and precious facet in the mosaic of ethnic groups which built America. I hope that this little volume may cast some light on their experience in the last frontier, Oklahoma, and inspire others to undertake more ambitious, comprehensive, and detailed studies. Most of their history remains unwritten. Consequently, I have found the help of many kind and knowledgeable people indispensable to my undertaking, and I remain deeply indebted to the following persons for their generous aid and counsel in making this work possible:

Mr. Delbert D. Amen Oklahoma City	Miss Rose Aul Enid
Mr. Arthur Appel Shattuck	The Rev. L. J. Becker Enid
Mrs. Edna May Armold El Reno	Mrs. Lois Belden Stillwater

Dr. Fred R. Belk
Sterling, Kansas

Mrs. Raymond L. Berry
Stillwater

Miss Lydia Bieberdorf
Stillwater

Mr. Earl D. Bierig
Okeene

Mrs. Edeltraut Bilger
Stillwater

Mr. John S. Butler
Stillwater

Dr. André P. DuChateau
Arkansas City, Kansas

Mr. and Mrs. J. G. Ehrlich
Shattuck

Mrs. Ella Ellis
Medford

Mr. Fred G. Fritzler
Woodward

Mr. Gus Friedemann
Stillwater

Mr. Raymond Geis
Cherokee

Mr. R. L. Geis
Gotebo

The Rev. and Mrs. G. L. Goertzen
Balko

Mr. Henry Graalman
Okeene

The Rev. Harry Haas
Okeene

Mrs. Alma Lea Hartman
Hooker

Mr. Emanuel Herbert
Breckinridge

Mr. and Mrs. H. G. Hohweiler
Fargo .

Mrs. H. H. Horn
Cordell

Mr. Peter M. Just
Fairview

Dr. Roy Just
Hillsboro, Kansas

Mr. and Mrs. Bill Karcher
Perry

Mr. and Mrs. R. J. Klaassen
Weatherford

Dr. Cornelius Krahn
North Newton, Kansas

Mr. and Mrs. George Krieger
Hobart

Miss Ottilia Laufer
Hobart

Mr. and Mrs. Aaron Lipps
Hobart

Mrs. Lillie Lipps
Okeene

Mrs. A. L. Lundgrin
Hooker

Mrs. Verda McGee
Cherokee

Mr. and Mrs. Eugene Martens
Hooker

Mr. Godfrey Martin
Buffalo

Mr. Lonnie Meissinger
Stillwater

Mr. Larry D. Miller
Stillwater

Mr. Glenn Mueller
Tulsa

Mr. and Mrs. Jake Mirtz
Enid

Mrs. Marie Oltmanns
Stillwater

Dr. Richard W. Payne
Oklahoma City

Mr. Gus Pekrul
Goltry

Mr. David C. Peters
Stillwater

Mrs. J. C. Pond
Medford

Mrs. Bernard H. Reding
El Reno

Mrs. Anneva Sander
Seiling

Miss Kay Schwendimann
Tulsa

Mrs. Lea Wahl
Fairview

Mr. Gary Watters
Stillwater

Mr. Henry Weber
Cherokee

The Rev. Walter Wehmeier
Perry

Mrs. Barbara Westfall
Okeene

Mr. Leo Winters
Oklahoma City

Mrs. Selma Witzke
Hooker

    Special thanks go to Dr. Vernon R. Wiebe and Professor Ray D. Lau, who not only provided valuable information concerning the subject of this book but also read the work in manuscript and gave me the benefit of their comments and insights. To Miss Ruth M. Amen, Executive Director, American Historical Society of Germans from Russia, and Mr. John F. Schmidt, Archivist, Mennonite Library and Archives, I shall be ever grateful for the access they gave me to their collections as well as for their encouragement of my efforts. The staffs of both the Edmon Low Library at Oklahoma State University and the Oklahoma Historical Society were unfailingly helpful and patient with my many requests. Mrs. Georganne Clark and Mr. Eldon Hardy turned my crude sketches into the clear and informative maps which accompany this volume, while Mrs. Barbara Adams typed the manuscript. Through the kindness of Mr. Francis Allai and Mr. James Van Houten of the U.S. Census Personal Service Branch, Pittsburg, Kansas, I was able to obtain much valuable data for which I am particularly indebted.

Finally, I owe a debt of gratitude to Dr. Anne Hodges Morgan, whose talents, leadership, and persistence made this series a reality, and to Dr. Kay Fagin, Director, Oklahoma Image, for her indispensable support and encouragement. With such colleagues and coworkers as these, the preparation of this book has been gratifying and pleasant. I hope that it will bring a similar pleasure to the reader.

Oklahoma State University   *Douglas Hale*

Chapter 1
THE OLD COUNTRY AND THE NEW LAND

Scattered across the vast landscapes of the Great Plains lie the homes of a people who share a heritage unsurpassed in the annals of pioneering: the Germans from Russia. Their pursuit of freedom, dedication to faith, and commitment to the principle that labor conquers all obstacles have uniquely prepared them to open new frontiers on four continents. They were among the first to settle western Oklahoma, bring its virgin sod under the plow, and turn its endless plains into a sea of wheat. The story of these first Russian-German pioneers—their adventures, incredible hardships, tragedies, and their ultimate success against formidable odds—provides the theme for this book.

As Oklahoma Territory was opened to white settlement after 1889, thousands of European immigrants took advantage of the singular opportunity which these millions of acres of new land afforded: to acquire a stake in the soil, to possess a farm of one's own. The largest proportion of the foreign-born immigrants to Oklahoma were German in language and culture, and most came from the new German Empire, only then flexing its power under Bismarck and William II. Still other German-speaking settlers had been born in Switzerland or Austria. There was another group of Germans, however, who differed from all the rest. For a century or more, these people had lived as foreign colonists in Russia, keeping to themselves, maintaining their own culture, language, and religion, and retaining an older, more traditional way of life than that of the modernized, urbanized, and industrialized Germans from Central Europe. The Germans from Russia spoke dialects which set them apart from the immigrants of the German Empire. In backward Russia they had missed many of the opportunities for economic advancement which were common in Western Europe. Moreover,

1

the Germans from Russia remained an agricultural people, while the other Germans tended to migrate to the cities and find industrial employment. On the Great Plains, therefore, the Russian Germans occupied a position quite distinct from the main body of German Americans.

In all, there were about 4,100 German immigrants from Russia living in Oklahoma at the time of statehood. As Map 1 indicates, they were dispersed widely throughout the western half of the state but often formed quite coherent communities of their own.[1] Each of these communities had its unique character and history, yet each illuminates the total experience of the people as a whole. It will be our task to examine individually the early years of these settlements, but before doing so it is useful to reflect upon the long and tortuous process by which the Russian-German pioneers found their way from the Rhine and the Volga to the banks of the Cimarron, the Washita, and the Canadian.[2]

Two centuries ago Russia was ruled by the shrewd and clever Catherine II (1762–96). During her reign, she added some 220,000 square miles of territory to her domain as a consequence of the absorption of Poland and victorious wars against the Turks. Most of these new territories were sparsely populated, unproductive, and vulnerable to hostile neighbors. Huge tracts of the older Russian lands were still virtually unoccupied, uncultivated, and ravaged by nomadic marauders. To render these territories productive and secure, the Czarina embarked upon an ambitious colonization program which would be continued and expanded by her successors well into the nineteenth century. During her reign, hundreds of thousands of Russian peasants were moved from the more crowded regions of her empire to the new lands. But Catherine also desired foreign colonists as well, since they would bring improved agricultural techniques and new skills to her backward land. In 1763 the Empress issued a manifesto designed to attract foreign immigrants into her domain. It promised the new settlers exemption from taxation and military service, religious liberty, local autonomy for their villages and schools, and best of all, free land. The Manifesto of 1763 proved a powerful magnet.[3]

Especially strong was its attraction to the inhabitants of the four-hundred-odd independent states which then comprised the territory of Germany. Because the petty German states were so divided against themselves, they served repeatedly as the tragic theater for all the major wars of the seventeenth and eighteenth centuries. The southwestern German states had suffered most grievously in the Seven Years' War, which ended the same year as Catherine's manifesto of invitation. Many other German states were to be invaded, devastated, and absorbed by more powerful neighbors in the course of the approaching conflicts ignited by the French Revolution and Napo-

Messer on the Volga. Courtesy AHSGR.

leon. This generation of destruction gave primary impetus for the immigration of thousands of Germans to Russia.

There were other inducements to leave as well. The peasants of western Germany suffered from a chronic shortage of land, which made famine a familiar horror. Oppressive rulers and harsh administrators exploited them shamelessly, and their sons were often conscripted and sold as soldiers by their sovereigns. The concept of freedom of religion was still unknown in most of Germany, and the petty princelings dictated and controlled the character of worship and belief.[4] There were, in short, more than adequate grounds to persuade these oppressed people to leave their villages along the Rhine in pursuit of an unknown future on the banks of the distant Volga. About 30,000 Germans, the vanguard of a great exodus, moved to Russia between 1764 and 1767.

Between 1786 and 1790, the immigration stream swelled still more as other thousands settled on the steppes of the southern

Ukraine. Catherine's grandson, Alexander I (1801–25), brought another flood of German colonists to the Empire after 1804. Most of these people came from the Danzig region of West Prussia and founded colonies along the northern littoral of the Black Sea. In all, between Catherine's manifesto and the gradual cessation of immigration after 1861, some 100,000 Germans made the arduous transition to peasant life in Russia.

Like most pioneers, they had their starving time. Their first years on the steppes were perilous and miserable; many would have fled back to Germany had they been able. The proverbial incompetence and corruption of the Russian bureaucracy left men, women, and children without food or shelter during the rib-cracking cold of the Russian winter in an area where the Volga remains frozen for 162 days in the year. Droughts and untimely frosts brought near starvation; epidemic disease raged through the isolated villages far from even the primitive medical care then available. The mortality was fearful: in 1817, fully one-third of the more than 10,000 immigrants to Russia died from an epidemic before reaching their destination. Brigands and outlaws on the frontier took a terrible toll. In 1774, for example, a Kirghiz raiding party tortured to death 150 inhabitants of the village of Mariental and carried off 300 others into slavery. On August 26, 1826, Kurdish brigands killed 30 and captured 140 of the residents of the Caucasus colony of Katherinenfeld. Russia could be a dangerous land.

But the German settlers eventually prospered and multiplied. Thrifty, hardworking, impressively prolific—families with fewer than eight living children were the exception—and superior farmers, these people struggled through the misery of the founding years to a modest level of security. By the end of the nineteenth century, approximately 1,750,000 Germans occupied more than 3,000 separate towns and villages stretching all the way from Bessarabia in the west to the middle Volga (Map 2). Though they accounted for less than 2 percent of the total population of Russia, they cultivated about 25 million acres of land (an area larger than Indiana). While many owned no land at all and were forced to eke out a living as farm laborers, the Germans tended to be more prosperous and progressive than the Russian peasants who surrounded them. The proportion of land in German hands was much larger than their percentage in the population. Although the Germans constituted only 8.8 percent of the population of Taurida Province, for example, they owned 38.3 percent of the farmland.

Their farms were concentrated in three major regions of European Russia. They established their westernmost colonies in Volhynia, a land of forest and marsh. Polish landlords had brought the first Germans into the region before it was annexed by Russia, but massive immigration did not begin until after the Napoleonic Wars. By 1914 some 200,000 Germans lived in the territory between Novograd-Volynski and Zhitomir. The second area was the most extensive, including the Black Sea littoral all the way from Bessarabia to the Sea of Azov. The first Germans came into this region shortly after Catherine's manifesto, but the real growth of these colonies began only after 1804. The Volga settlements, constituting the third region, consisted of 195 towns and villages inhabited by more than half a million people by 1914. Centering on Saratov, these colonies lay on both the Hill Side *("Bergseite")*, or west bank of the great river, and the Meadow Side *("Wiesenseite")* to the east. Most of the original Volga Germans had come from Hesse and the Rhenish Palatinate. Though there were other scattered colonies from St. Petersburg *(Leningrad)* to Central Asia, the vast majority of Germans lived in the three areas defined above.

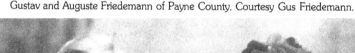

Gustav and Auguste Friedemann of Payne County. Courtesy Gus Friedemann.

These colonists did not reside in isolated homesteads as in America but in self-contained villages surrounded by the land they cultivated. For a century after their original settlement, the Russian government, though the most autocratic in Europe, allowed the colonists to exercise a high degree of freedom in their own local affairs. Despite occasional meddling by officious bureaucrats, the Germans were able to choose their own leaders through the process of town meetings. Moreover, their villages were deliberately cut off from the Russian population of the surrounding area. Some economic contact existed, but there was very little social or cultural interchange. Most Germans never learned Russian. They maintained their own schools and churches and assiduously perpetuated their language.

The original plan for foreign colonization had stipulated that the Germans were to be segregated according to religion; each colony was to maintain but a single church. This principle was followed throughout the life of the colonies. Lutherans and members of the Reformed Church were referred to collectively as "Evangelicals" and administered as a single religious body. They constituted 80 percent of the German population, while 13.5 percent were Roman Catholic. A few colonies counted members of several different faiths, but in general the principle of religious exclusivity was followed throughout the nineteenth century. The Volga town of Stephan, for example, was Evangelical; only nine miles away lay Leichting, which, though founded at the same time as Stephan, was wholly Catholic.

Although the Mennonites constituted but 3.7 percent of the German-speaking population of Russia at the end of the nineteenth century, they deserve special consideration since so many came to the United States. With considerable justification, the Russian government treated them as a separate ethnic group distinct from the other German colonists, and they tended to be among the most prosperous of the foreign settlers. The Mennonite faith had originated in Switzerland during the Reformation of the sixteenth century. Strictly literalistic in their interpretation of Scripture, the Mennonites developed a doctrine that called upon the faithful to live apart from a world steeped in sin. Thus, they renounced participation in political affairs and refused any form of military service. Their advocacy of adult baptism, nonviolence, and congregational autonomy made them victims of cruel persecution by both Catholic and Protestant authorities alike until the faith was practically wiped out in Switzerland. By 1530, however, the movement had migrated down the Rhine to Holland, where it struck deep roots in spite of violent persecution.

6

Here Menno Simons (1496–1561) formalized the doctrine of the sect and gave it his name. In an effort to escape martyrdom and bloodshed, Dutch Mennonites took refuge in the marshy wastes of the Vistula Delta near Danzig about 1550. These pious and hard-working Dutch peasants drained the marshes and turned the land into productive farms and prosperous villages.

In the process of creating this community, however, the Mennonites gradually abandoned their Dutch language and embraced the Low German dialect common to the region. When their lands came under Prussian control in 1772, the impositions, restrictions, and discriminations enacted against them became so burdensome that several thousand elected to emigrate to Russia. Under a special dispensation of rights and privileges, the first Mennonites settled in the czarist empire in 1788. By 1914 they numbered about 104,000 and dwelled in some 400 villages concentrated in two areas of the Ukraine: the Chortitza region of the lower Dnieper and along the Molotschna River, sixty miles north of the Sea of Azov. The Mennonites, a people of predominately Dutch ancestry who had acquired German language and culture in the course of their historic wanderings, always remained somewhat apart from the other Germans in Russia.

By the middle of the nineteenth century, the German colonists had become the most advanced and progressive agrarian group in Russia. Most families, though by no means wealthy, owned at least a little land, and a few individuals had become prosperous grain merchants, mill operators, and farm equipment manufacturers. They had introduced improved breeds of cattle, developed orchards and vineyards, and afforested millions of acres. Their villages and towns were neat, orderly, and attractive, and their separate school system was far superior to anything Russia had seen. By 1897, when the illiteracy rate for Russia as a whole stood at 79 percent, almost all the German colonists could at least read.

So they prospered. But beginning about 1870, this prospect of success and bright promise was clouded by three developments which in the next generation would persuade hundreds of thousands of Germans to abandon their hard-won homes and emigrate to America. In the first place, the enormous social and economic changes wrought by Czar Alexander II (1855–81) in his efforts to modernize Russia began to imperil seriously the security of the Germans. In 1861 the Czar had liberated millions of Russian serfs, and this made necessary a whole catalogue of legal and social innovations to adjust the country to this fundamental transformation of society. Henceforth, the Germans were to be treated no differently from the newly liberated serfs; one by one, they lost the privileges accorded them by Catherine. In 1871 the government abrogated the "perpetual" exemption from military service which the colonists had hitherto enjoyed. Several years later their towns and villages lost the right of self-government and were brought under direct state control. The Russian Ministry of Education took over the supervision of their schools, though German remained the language of instruction until 1914.

In part, all of this represented the inevitable consequences of efforts by a great nation to modernize itself and integrate all its inhabitants into a unified society. But it was also the result of an ever-intensifying policy of Russification by the government. Hostility and suspicion toward everything German and popular envy against that minority for their superior status increased especially after the accession of Czar Alexander III (1881–94) to the throne. Since anti-German prejudice was deliberately fostered by high authorities in the state, many Germans came to believe that their culture, religion, and language were doomed to be drowned in the Russian sea around them. In the end, this premonition was prophetic.

Finally, the German colonists faced an economic dilemma for which there was no solution but emigration: a shortage of land. The original grants of land to the colonies had been adequate for the modest population which had first settled them, but as the population expanded there was simply not enough to go around. On the Hill Side of the Volga, for instance, there had once been forty to forty-five acres available for every male colonist; by 1860, there were only four. Rents consequently rose beyond the capacity of the landless to pay them. For many there was no alternative but to leave.

Actuated by such considerations, perhaps as many as 300,000 of the German colonists chose to emigrate, beginning in 1873. Two factors especially attracted them to the United States: the Homestead Act of 1862 which made free land available to farmers who would cultivate it, and the absence of military conscription. The majority of these immigrants to America preferred to settle on the Great Plains, whose terrain and climate resembled that which they left in Russia and where arable land could still be had for homesteading. More than half found their way to five states: North and South Dakota, Nebraska, Colorado, and Kansas.

Most of the Germans from Russia who eventually migrated to

Oklahoma had settled originally in Kansas and Nebraska. Two areas of concentration developed in Kansas during the 1870s. The first, focusing upon Marion, Harvey, and McPherson counties, included a very high proportion of Mennonites. These three Kansas counties would supply the great majority of the eager Russian-German home-steaders who moved into Oklahoma Territory after 1889. A second Kansas enclave, centering on Ellis, Russell, and Rush counties, was settled primarily by Catholics and Evangelicals. Nebraska had a high concentration of Germans from Russia in the southeast quadrant of the state, between Hastings and Lincoln, and in the extreme west, around Scottsbluff. These new settlers built their houses of sod and attacked the prairie with their plows as their great-grandfathers had broken the steppe a century before. After untold hardships, privation, and unremitting labor—in spite of drought, cyclone, blizzard, hail, and 'hoppers—they began to prosper. It was the Germans from Russia who inaugurated the extensive cultivation of winter wheat in the region, turning the Great Plains into the granary of the world.[5]

The Germans from Russia who settled in the plains states after 1873 were marked by three salient characteristics which they retained to a large degree as they eventually made their way to Oklahoma. These were "the three Fs": farming, faith, and family. Unlike many American immigrants, such as Italians and Jews, for example, the Germans from Russia avoided the cities and remained upon the land. Agriculture was their way of life, and they clung to the farm as long as it was possible. They also remained a profoundly religious people, and the churches they transplanted from the old country became the nuclei around which their communities coalesced. Finally, they retained the extended family as a basic social unit in the face of American mobility and rapid change. For the most part they came to America as members of large family groups from the same Russian village. Here they perpetuated these familial and community ties by settling near each other and establishing churches as similar as possible to those they had left behind.

Originally, many of these immigrants had envisioned their exis-tence in the United States to be what it had been in Russia: that of a separate people, living their own lives and following their own ways apart from the larger society around them. It was not long, however, before the forces of American mobility and assimilation caught up with them and revealed this expectation to be an illusion. Land-holding patterns in the United States, whereby each family occupied 160 acres of land for its own, made their old-country village life impossible except in a few rare instances. Most of the Kansas and Nebraska Germans from Russia had chosen land along the great trunk railways of the country—at the same time both the symbols and primary instruments of American mobility. The public school system brought their children immediately into the mainstream of English-speaking society. Besides, America was far more the land of opportunity than Russia had ever been, and opportunity makes for change, ambition, and social mobility. So while these early Russian-German communities prospered and flourished, more and more of their young people looked beyond the family farmstead for their own stake in the soil.

Thus, when the federal government began opening the lands of Oklahoma to white settlement in 1889, thousands of these young farmers saw it as a godsend. At that time, farmland in Kansas was fetching $20 per acre, a price far beyond the resources of most young immigrants who wanted to found a farm and a family. For a modest filing fee, anyone who could work, who could endure the hardships of pioneering, and who had faith in himself could make his way in the new land of Oklahoma.

Settlers poured into the Territory in pulsating surges as a series of thirteen separate tracts were successively opened through the process of run, lottery, or purchase. From 1889 down to statehood in 1907, Oklahoma Territory presented an incredible spectacle. No sooner had one enormous tract been thrown open to homesteaders, given some semblance of political order, and provided with a rudimentary economic infrastructure, than millions of new acres were opened nearby in which the whole process was repeated. Five of these openings were most important in the settlement of the state because of the vastness of the lands made available. The so-called Unassigned Lands in central Oklahoma were opened by the prototypical Run of April 22, 1889. The Panhandle, or "No Man's Land" as it was affectionately called, became available for settlement in 1890, but few homesteaders took advantage of this opportunity until a decade later. The government threw open the lands once reserved for the Cheyenne and Arapaho Indians in the Run of April 19, 1892. The greatest race of all took place on September 16, 1893, with the Cherokee Outlet Run. Finally, a government lottery opened the Comanche, Kiowa, and Apache lands in the southwest between June 9 and August 6, 1901.

We shall follow the wanderings of the Germans from Russia as they entered these new territories one by one. First, let us turn to

10

Douglas Hale

those who settled the Unassigned Lands in central Oklahoma. From there, we must look to the southwest, toward the Washita River and the Wichita Mountains. Finally, northwestern Oklahoma—the Cherokee Outlet and No Man's Land—will be the setting for our saga.

Among the sixty thousand or so who participated in that wild scramble for claims to the Unassigned Lands in 1889 were a number of adventurous young Russian-Germans who would found the first two communities of their ethnic group in the state. About eight miles north of present-day El Reno, a party of Mennonites filed for homesteads on the western edge of the Unassigned Lands. These pioneers, including the Penner and Warkentin families, were attracted to the area because of its proximity to the Mennonite mission at Darlington in the Cheyenne-Arapaho Reservation just to the west. In 1891 these settlers founded the Mennoville Church, the first Mennonite church in Oklahoma. Though its congregation disbanded in 1952, the original building still stands as a monument to these pioneers.[6]

On the northern edge of the Unassigned Lands, in Payne County, another group of Germans from Russia established a community near Marena, about nine miles west of Stillwater, in 1889. These people came from the Russian province of Volhynia, and their experience illustrated how families followed individuals, villages followed families, and regions followed villages into the new land. Volhynia had once been part of Poland, and wealthy Polish landowners had first brought Germans into the region to increase the productivity of their huge estates. After Russia annexed the area in 1793, German immigration increased. During the years after 1861 the emancipation of the serfs left the landlords without a supply of cheap labor, and many were forced to sell their land at bargain prices. This windfall attracted a further flood of German immigrants. By 1897, there were 171,331 Germans living in 139 villages clustered between Novograd-Volynski and Zhitomir, west of Kiev. Their industriousness had made the region one of the richest in Russia. But because they occupied an exposed frontier province, the Volhynian Germans were among the first to feel the effects of the anti-German policies inaugurated after 1881 by the Czar. They were discriminated against economically and culturally; landlords frequently evicted without notice those who were renting land. Consequently, a very large proportion of these people chose to emigrate. Most who settled in America favored the forested lands of Michigan and Wisconsin which reminded them of their homeland.

A few, however, drifted farther south. Among them were various

11

members of the Friedemann and Bieberdorf families, both from the Volhynian village of Annette and both to become prominent leaders of the Russian-German community in western Payne County. Annette had been founded in 1816 in the wooded valley of the Zjerem River. By 1890 the population consisted of about twenty families who lived in modest thatch-roofed cottages of clay or wood. The villagers cultivated wheat, barley, and sugar beets by hand and sold their produce to Jewish merchants in the market town of Novograd-Volynski, some six miles away. Several local millers and a blacksmith supplied Annette's basic needs, while other necessities the inhabitants might purchase from peddlers. The heart of their community and the pride of their village was the austere but imposing Lutheran Church, built of wood in 1818. Though the presence of an ordained pastor in the village was rare and irregular, a lay preacher held services every week and kept school besides.

Four years after the colony was founded, the Widow Bieberdorf and her two sons migrated from Bohnsack, a fishing village on the Baltic coast near Danzig, and settled in Annette. From these seeds the Bieberdorf family sprouted in Russia. Like their neighbors, they drained the surrounding marshes, cleared the land, and carved homes in the wilderness. The family prospered and became the owners of a windmill in the village. In the 1880s, two young scions of the family, Edward and Friedrich, immigrated to Harvey County, Kansas. After the Run of '89, both young men homesteaded quarter sections in Payne County, about nine miles west of Stillwater.

They were soon followed by their kinsman from Annette, Adolph Bieberdorf, who was thirty years old, married, and the father of four children. He was able to buy a relinquishment near his fellow countrymen in July, 1890, and began learning to farm American style. Like Squanto, who had initiated another earlier group of newcomers, the Pilgrims, into the mysteries of New World agriculture, a Negro neighbor explained to him that corn should be planted "when the oak leaves are the size of a squirrel's ear." Bieberdorf also learned to cultivate cotton, a crop unknown to the peasants of Volhynia. The folks back home were puzzled by the plant, since its German name *Baumwolle* (literally, "tree-wool"), conjured up images of huge trees bedecked with fleece. To clarify this misconception, Bieberdorf had a cotton stalk photographed as part of the family portrait to send back home to Russia.[7]

Their community grew. Within two years following the Run, more than a dozen Volhynian families had moved into the area, and the hamlet of Marena grew up to serve their needs. Among the more recent immigrants was the family of Robert Friedemann, also from Annette. His ancestors had originally plied their trade as textile machine mechanics in Halle, Saxony, but had migrated eastward to accompany the expansion of the cloth industry across Europe. From the Lodz district of Poland, Robert Friedemann's father had moved farther east to Annette where he purchased land in 1869. Here he and his wife reared five sons and three daughters. The eldest son, Paul, was conscripted into the Russian Army in 1884. Two other brothers would eventually be drafted as well. Robert, the second son, had other ideas, however.

The Adolph Bieberdorf family. Courtesy of Miss Lydia Bieberdorf.

In July, 1889, Robert Friedemann and his young wife Lydia immigrated to Halstead, Kansas, where he found a job on the railroad and she took in washing. But Oklahoma beckoned. Their pastor, Reverend J. V. Kauffeld of Newton, Kansas, had made a ministerial tour through the Payne County area in 1890, and he recommended this vicinity to the couple. Besides, Lydia's half brother, Edward Bieberdorf, was already established in the Marena community. In

1891 the Friedemanns joined the Bieberdorfs in their two-room cabin in Payne County. Before long, Robert was able to buy land of his own. In 1892 he and his neighbors from Volhynia founded a church, one of the first Lutheran churches in the state. Informal services were initially held in a school. Two years later the Peace Church was chartered by the German Evangelical Synod of North America, and in 1897 its parishioners built their first building. It became the nucleus for the present Salem Lutheran Church of Stillwater.[8]

In the meantime, other friends and family members from Russia joined the community. Perhaps the most notable of these early pioneers was Robert Friedemann's elder brother, Paul. He had been born in 1861 in a Podolian village and as a child accompanied his mother and father in their move to Annette. A sickly boy, he developed early a keen sense of duty and religious dedication; these remained with him as he grew into a robust young man. Paul Friedemann was conscripted into the Russian Army at twenty-three and used the opportunity to obtain a medical education at the military medical institute. Assigned to a cavalry regiment, the quiet, devout young doctor appeared an anomaly among his hard-drinking comrades, but he won their respect nonetheless. After his active duty was completed in 1890, he was relieved to return to civilian life.

That same year he married Emilie Bergstrasser and began the practice of medicine near Annette, where he remained for three years. But this period coincided with an intensification of the anti-German policies by the government, and Dr. Friedemann came to feel that neither his faith nor his future was secure in Russia. Soon he had children to consider as well. As a result, the enthusiastic letters from his brother extolling the opportunities of Oklahoma Territory found a receptive hearing. Paul, his wife, and his parents resolved to join Robert Friedemann in America.

The doctor was able to secure an exit permit on the pretext of accompanying his wife to Germany for medical treatment—a bit of deception which troubled his conscience for years—and the family set out in the fall of 1893. They traveled by way of Hamburg and Galveston, and the voyage was rough and miserable for the entire family. Almost all their luggage was stolen en route; by the time they arrived at Galveston, they were ill and weakened by the ordeal. The hardships of the journey were such that all three of the Friedemann children died before the family had fully settled into its new home in Payne County.

That winter on the Oklahoma prairie was a dismal one. Moreover, Paul Friedemann soon realized that the sparse population of the Marena community could not support a physician. There were other possibilities, however. Western Kingfisher County had been opened to settlement the year before, and there was a growing German community about ten miles northwest of the county seat. They needed a doctor, and Friedemann was intrigued by the possibility of founding a German town on the frontier. He and his wife moved to the new settlement in 1894, and led in the formation of the town of Kiel (Loyal). Dr. Friedemann became its first postmaster and physician.

Kiel gradually acquired stores, churches, the obligatory town band, and about 200 inhabitants. Friedemann became its most prominent citizen. His practice throve as he traveled by horse and buggy to visit patients within a thirty-mile radius. Medicine on the frontier was eventful, exciting, and occasionally even dangerous, as when outlaws on the run required his services. Through periodic refresher courses in Chicago, the doctor kept abreast of advancements in the profession and became well known in medical circles throughout the territory. His family was growing: Friedemann and his wife became the parents of five children while at Kiel. His personal affairs were prospering as well, and the doctor bought a farm and hired a man to run it. But at last the tasks involved in meeting all these various responsibilites became too much for the couple.

At the age of forty-five, Friedemann gave up his post office and

Left: Dr. Paul Friedemann. Courtesy of Dr. André DuChateau. Right: Fred Meissinger from *Messer on the Volga*; settled at Kiel (Loyal), Oklahoma. Courtesy of Lonnie Meissinger.

15

his farming, moved his family back to Payne County, and confined his efforts to a medical practice in Stillwater. "Dr. Paul" became a local institution. His elegant, courtly manner, pride in his German culture and church, distinctive style, and ready wit were proverbial. For thirty-eight years he served the town of Stillwater, and though dead for more than a generation, he is still remembered with affection and respect.[9]

Like Paul Friedemann, many of the original settlers of the Unassigned Lands were lured to other areas of Oklahoma Territory as the successive openings gave promise of greener pastures and greater opportunities farther afield. The next major tract to be thrown open to the eager homesteaders was the Cheyenne-Arapaho Reservation in 1892. Hundreds of Germans from Russia poured into this section of the embryonic state, and their story, too, was dramatic.

Chapter 2

FROM THE WASHITA RIVER
TO THE WICHITA MOUNTAINS

The United States Government set aside the west-central region of Oklahoma in 1869 as a home for the Cheyenne and Arapaho. The army moved about 3,500 Indians into this reservation and established an agency at Darlington, a few miles northwest of what would become El Reno. Only twenty-three years later, however, the government opened this tract of some three million acres to white settlement. Among those who homesteaded this area in 1892 were a host of Germans from Russia, who would here establish some of their most important communities.

Like the founders of Mennoville, many of the original pioneers were first attracted to the Cheyenne-Arapaho country by the Mennonite missionaries who had ministered to the Indians at the Darlington Agency since 1880. Their story is in itself an intriguing saga, sufficient to inspire one of the great novelists of the nineteenth century, Theodor Fontane, to deal with the theme.[1] Of all those who served at Darlington Mission, one man stood out as perhaps the most complex and interesting figure. His name was Heinrich R. Voth, and his life epitomized many aspects of the Russian-German experience.

Voth was born in the village of Alexanderwohl, one of the Mennonite colonies on the Molotschna River, in 1855. He came from a poor family; his father owned no land himself but earned a living as a cabinetmaker and farm hand. When Heinrich was nine years old, his parents moved to the newly founded village of Gnadenthal, five miles away, where his father was given land in return for the toilsome task of building farms and beginning the cultivation of the virgin steppe. Their son thus became familiar with the rigors of pioneering at a tender age. He much preferred, however, the village school, the books he eagerly devoured, and the church. A studious lad, Heinrich showed a marked facility for languages. He was also deeply religious and fascinated by the missionary emphasis of his church. These inclinations were to shape the direction of his life.

In 1874, virtually the entire congregation. of the Alexanderwohl Church, including young Voth and his family, immigrated to Kansas. Upon arrival, they were temporarily housed in the shops of the Santa Fe Railway until members of the congregation bought land (at about $2.50 per acre) a dozen miles north of Newton, Kansas. Here they established the new Alexanderwohl Mennonite Church. In the complicated process of buying land, procuring supplies, and learning a new mode of agriculture, the Mennonites were desperate for someone to act as translator and interpreter. Heinrich Voth, only 19, now came into his own. He had studied English in Russia; it required but a few weeks in Kansas for him to become fluent in the language. He scurried from family to family and into the town of Newton, opening accounts, buying farm equipment and livestock, scrutinizing contracts, and making himself generally indispensable.

A bright boy like young Voth could not escape the notice of one of Newton's more enterprising merchants, who gave him a job in his store. Heinrich was so successful at this that within a year he considered going into business for himself. But then "the Lord took hold" and cast the youth into an entirely different way of life. Voth's Mennonite neighbors virtually drafted him to serve as the teacher for their first school; at 21, he proceeded to "crucify the merchant" in himself. From teaching it was but a short step to embarking upon the career of a missionary. In 1877 he began ministerial studies in Ohio and then completed his training at the St. Louis Medical College. By 1882 Voth was ready for his first assignment in the mission field.[2]

The Mennonite Board of Missions assigned him to serve as a teacher under S. S. Haury, superintendent of the recently established mission to the Cheyenne and Arapaho at Darlington. For this idealistic young man of twenty-seven, the circumstances surrounding his assignment were not particularly auspicious. In February, 1882, the new Indian boarding school had burned down, killing four children including Haury's own infant son. Many of Voth's Indian charges had been actively at war with the United States Army only a few years before, and the Cheyennes especially resisted white efforts to deprive them of their freedom, their land, and their way of life. During the ten years which Voth would spend at Darlington, he would serve under five different agents—men who had little in common besides their proclivity to deplore the mistakes of their predecessors. The task assigned him was impossible since official Indian policy held that the proud nomadic hunters of the buffalo were to be turned into settled and successful farmers almost overnight. Toward· this end, and incidentally to make the reservation land available for white settlement, the Government extinguished tribal title to the soil and dispersed and scattered the Indians to their separate and individual allotments. All these factors combined to make Voth's ministry an exceedingly difficult one.

But despite these enormous problems and his never-ending burden of work, Voth became the model of a dedicated and untiring missionary. He helped rebuild the school at Darlington; he opened another mission school at Cantonment (near present Canton); he helped found a demonstration farm and mission station at Shelly, on the Washita River sixty miles to the southwest. He bent every effort to teach the Indian children basic farming and homemaking skills as well as the rudiments of reading, writing, and numbers. Slowly the regularity of their attendance at his school improved, and he was named superintendent of the mission. Despite setbacks and disappointments, the young missionary could take pride in the fact that willingly or not, the Indians were being forced to follow the "white man's road."

For Voth fully shared the ruling doctrine that the Indian could survive and progress only at the cost of repudiating his entire culture. He required the school children to speak only English. He expressed scorn for their "heathenish" ways, and as a zealous Christian, he was dedicated to the extirpation of their religion and ritual life. Voth complained that the Indians' persistence in their pernicious festivals and dances "undermined" his work. He advised his superiors that "the Indians ought to be compelled more to turn a new leaf." He rejoiced that their "heathenish customs [had] been undermined and partly discontinued" as a result of his labors and looked forward to the extinction of tribal title to the land. For as he correctly predicted, "by the breaking up of the tribal relation of these Indians, a great many of their old customs will be discontinued."[3]

How strange to discover, therefore, that this same man went to enormous pains to learn the Arapaho language; that he observed and studied their dances and customs with avid interest; that he took copious notes and published detailed and authoritative accounts of Indian folkways in the most learned of journals! How paradoxical

19

that this hostile observer who so often expressed abhorrence at the "heathenish" practices of the Indians was at the same time recording their tales and legends to preserve them, even as their way of life neared extinction.[4] With one part of his being Voth strove to replace the "inferior" culture of the Indian with that of his own; with the other, he directed enormous energy and talent toward the study and preservation of that dying culture.

This paradox would extend into his next assignment. In 1884 Voth had married Barbara Baer of Summerfield, Kansas, and brought her to Darlington. Five years later she died, leaving him the care of a small daughter. In order to make provision for this child, and with his own health undermined by the rigors of missionary life, Voth obtained a leave of absence in 1892. He used this respite to recoup his health and visit his old home in Russia. Upon his return, he married Martha Moser, an Ohio girl who had been a fellow mission worker at Darlington. At this point, the Board of Missions challenged him with a new assignment: first Mennonite missionary to the Hopis of Arizona. With his new wife and his daughter, Voth took up this task in July, 1893.

He chose to set up his headquarters at Oraibi, the chief village of the Hopi, 35 miles from the government agency at Keams Canyon, 75 miles from the closest white settlement, and 125 miles from the nearest railroad. To Voth and his wife fell the full task of building a mission station. The couple were allotted $650 with which they were to construct a house, a barn, and a chapel. Skilled at carpentry, Voth soon had a habitable dwelling for his family. He dug his own well. It was also part of his job to raise corn and vegetables in the sterile sand at the foot of the mesa. His first responsibility, of course, was to save souls, and Voth went about it with his usual obsessive dedication. To be an effective missionary, he felt, required him to learn the Hopi language, and this he mastered without great difficulty. But he was also convinced that he must become familiar with the intricate ceremonial life of the Hopi, their religion, and their culture. Voth was fascinated: *"What a pantheon, what a religious system, what a rich language, what traditions, what organization!"* he exclaimed.[5]

Once again, he was caught in the old dilemma: the more success he enjoyed as a missionary, the more he undermined a complex way of life which he found both intriguing and worthy of respect. Voth collected artifacts and sacred objects; he gained admittance to the sacrosanct kivas; he observed and recorded all aspects of Hopi life. By 1899 he was such an authority that the Field Museum of Chicago

The Reverend Heinrich R.
Voth and daughter on the
Hopi Indian Reservation.
Courtesy of Dr. Richard
Payne.

commissioned him to set up its Hopi exhibit. Later the Fred Harvey
hotel chain employed him to create the Hopi House on the rim of
Grand Canyon. Between 1901 and 1912 he published ten major
monographs—almost a thousand pages in all—on Hopi ceremonials
and customs. The Hopi called him *Kihakaumta:* "One who digs
among Old Ruins."[6] No one contributed more to the preservation of
Hopi culture than Voth.

But he was also one of the instruments of its destruction. The
missionary brought his alien and disruptive faith to the land of the
Hopi at a critical time in their history. The founding of a government
agency and reservation had broken the isolation of their fragile
culture. In 1894 the government attempted to extinguish tribal owner-
ship in favor of individual property allotments, and four years later
began forcing Hopi children to attend the white man's schools.
Finally, in 1898, a disastrous smallpox epidemic wiped out about
one-fifth of the 2,200 inhabitants of the reservation. The upshot of
all these pressures was a schism within the tribe between the so-
called "friendlies," who were ready to walk the "white man's road,"
and the "hostiles," who clung stubbornly to the old ways and
resisted every innovation. Ceremonialism broke down, Old Oraibi was
virtually depopulated, and Hopi culture was corrupted by alien
influences.

It was against this background that Voth labored. Though he treated the Indians when they were sick and defended them against the more egregious acts of government coercion, some of the Hopis came to hate and resent him for his prying ways. One recalled: "He always pushed to the front, anywhere he wanted to be, even in the kivas. Nobody could stop him. One time a Two Horn priest tried to stop him from going into a kiva. He kicked the Two Horn priest out of the way and went in."[7] Many were offended when he exposed the sacred relics of the tribe to the profane gaze of the museum-goers: he had betrayed the esoteric mysteries of their faith. On the other hand, the Board of Missions did not find Voth's work at Oraibi satisfactory either. Although a few Hopis loved and befriended him, he made but a handful of converts during his nine years on the reservation. Lightning struck the chapel that Voth had built on the mesa, and the Indians avoided it as a place accursed. Torn as he was between the scientific curiosity of the ethnographer and the religious zeal of the missionary, Voth was able to satisfy neither party.

His sojourn at Oraibi ended tragically. Mrs. Voth died in childbirth in 1901, and the widower now had four small children to look after. He returned to Newton the following year and henceforth divided his time between his ethnographical studies and more conventional pastoral duties for his church. From 1914 until his retirement in 1927 he served as resident minister for the Zoar Mennonite Church at Goltry, Oklahoma. He died in 1931.

Voth's younger colleague in the mission field, John J. Kliewer, was superintendent of the Cheyenne mission at Cantonment, near present-day Canton. He would be instrumental in establishing the most numerous concentration of Germans from Russia in Oklahoma, those who settled in Washita County. Like Voth, Kliewer had been born in the Molotschna region of South Russia. In 1889 he and his brother Henry founded a mission station at Shelly, on the Washita River, to serve a settlement of Indians nearby. But the territory was opened to white homesteaders three years later, and most of the Indians moved out of the area to claim their individual allotments. Effective missionary activity became impossible at the Shelly site.

Still, Kliewer was reluctant to lose the improvements he had made on the land, so he bought the quarter section upon which the mission stood. The Run of 1892 had left many of the surrounding tracts unclaimed, and there was still much vacant land in the area. Kliewer therefore urged his coreligionists in Kansas to move south and take advantage of this abundant opportunity. In the fall of 1892

Kliewer's brother guided a group of Russian Mennonites from Buhler, Kansas, to a tract about five miles northwest of Shelly Mission. They filed their claims, and in March, 1893, thirteen families moved to this area a few miles west of the present town of Corn. Additional families poured in, and by 1894 they had already organized two Mennonite churches nearby.[8]

For one group of immigrants in particular, the new colony was especially attractive. They were the destitute veterans of the Great Trek of the Russian Mennonites to central Asia, actors in a saga as colorful and dramatic as any in the annals of pioneering. A strange destiny would bring these wanderers from the banks of the Amu Darya in distant Turkestan to the Washita Valley of Oklahoma. Let us examine the force of that destiny in the life of one man, Jacob Klaassen (1867-1948).

Of Dutch ancestry, Klaassen's Mennonite forebears had migrated to West Prussia in the early eighteenth century, where they remained for a hundred and fifty years. In 1853 Jacob's father, a schoolmaster, moved to Russia and settled in the new village of Köppental, near Samara (Kuibyshev) on the Volga. Here his son Jacob was born in 1867. Köppental was a pleasant village of twenty-five families, and Jacob enjoyed an idyllic boyhood, playing along the brook which flowed beside its neat farms. He would in later years recall the memories "of the quiet summer evenings when the village shepherd would drive the cattle into the village, every animal finding its own gate. A more beautiful picture of peaceful village life there never was."[9]

Köppental had an excellent school and a fine church. But it was torn by doctrinal strife. In the 1870s the forces of change began to stir the religious restlessness of a number of pietistic Mennonite congregations in both the Volga region and the Ukraine. Recent immigrants from Prussia, moreover, had brought with them a fervent millenarianism which proclaimed that the Second Coming of Christ was at hand. Köppental lay at the heart of this eschatological ferment which ultimately split the community. By the summer of 1880, Claasz Epp, Jr., a charismatic combination of practical farmer and prophetic visionary, had persuaded 159 Mennonite families from the Ukraine and the Volga that their duty lay in undertaking a pilgrimage to distant Turkestan to make ready a place for the Returning Lord somewhere south of Samarkand.[10]

The Czar had only recently annexed the vast desert basin of Turkestan to his domains. Half the size of the United States, most of it was wild, bleak, and virtually uninhabitable. But Epp convinced his followers that there they could find not only the millenium but abundant land and exemption from the Russian draft as well. Thus inspired, the pilgrims set out in five separate wagon trains across the forbidding deserts and precipitous gorges of Central Asia toward Tashkent, some 1,400 miles away. Jacob's father had been among the first who elected to follow Epp in his search for the Returning Christ.

. Jacob was thirteen years old on that August morning in 1880 when his father's wagon fell in line and turned toward their distant goal. At first the boy enjoyed the excitement of travel and marveled at the sights along the way: the camel caravans which conveyed the pilgrims across the desert, the colorful costumes and customs of the Kirghiz nomads who guided them, and the polychrome Tomb of Tamerlane at Samarkand (Map 3). But their dream of a promised land soon turned into a nightmare.

The land the Mennonites had been promised proved sterile and worthless. The Russian government now threatened to draft all their young men. More than a thousand miles from home, with their supplies at the point of exhaustion, the immigrants were reduced to wandering from one encampment to the next, decimated by typhoid, terrorized by brigands, victimized by local rulers, and dispirited by the harsh and unyielding climate. Overcome by disease, exposure, and privation, both Jacob's father and his elder sister died in 1881, leaving only Jacob and his brother Michael to look after their mother. After two years of unspeakable hardship, the desperate migrants found a temporary haven on the marshy, vermin-infested bank of the Amu Darya. Jacob describes their situation upon arrival in this wilderness: "Here we sat with our things, under an open sky in a robber-infested region far from any culturally advanced settlement, many hundred *wersts* from any fellow believers, and generally removed from all civilization."[11]

Slowly the beleaguered survivors began to create a civilization of their own: they laid out a village, drained marshes, cleared fields, planted crops, and undertook a brave new beginning. But they were trapped. The area was terrorized by Turkmen bandits who raided the settlement repeatedly, stole their livestock, and murdered their people. If the Mennonites did not fight back, they would be destroyed; if they defended themselves, they would violate an essential tenet of their creed—nonviolence. As young as Jacob was, even he could recognize the dilemma: "Not only was our existence in question . . .

but a basic principle of our faith, non-resistance. Therefore, we could not stay here."[12] Thus, after four years of unrelieved misery, about one-third of the Turkestan pilgrims at last became disillusioned with their prophet's increasing fanaticism and resolved to seek a new refuge in a better land: America.

In the spring of 1884 thirty-eight destitute families left Turkestan behind. Through the aid of their coreligionists in the United States, these Mennonites came to Kansas and Nebraska to begin a new life. Widow Klaassen and her two sons joined those refugees who were brought to Beatrice, Nebraska. The new beginning was hard, however. They came with virtually nothing; life was difficult, and the cost of land was high in the prairie states. For the young men, the chance to own a farm and found a family seemed remote indeed. Between the ages of eighteen and twenty-seven Jacob worked as a farm hand in Nebraska. Then he and his brother heard about the Washita Valley in Oklahoma, where free land was still available.

Mr. and Mrs. Jake Bierig of Isabella. Courtesy of Earl D. Bierig.

In 1894 Jacob and Michael Klaassen took up homesteads near Shelly, as did dozens of other impoverished veterans of the Turkestan trek. Even in their new homes, they continued to cling together: Of the forty-six charter members of the Herold Mennonite Church near Bessie, thirty-six had made the Turkestan journey.

Now with his own farm and in the midst of old friends and neighbors, Jacob could establish a family. In 1895 he married a girl from Newton, Kansas, and took her to her new home—a sod barn. Through unremitting labor the couple wrenched a living from their frontier farm and began to prosper. By 1903 Jacob could at last provide his wife with a frame house. Six sons were born to the couple, and both Jacob and his brother served their church as ministers. It required all his profound faith for Jacob to endure the losses of the following years, however. Both his young wife and his infant daughter died in 1908; a son was killed in a tragic farm accident; Jacob himself almost died from encephalitis. Yet, by the time he was forty-five he had recovered from these blows and was a prosperous farmer.[13]

But the First World War brought trouble from an unexpected direction. In the climate of war-born hysteria following the American declaration of war against Germany in 1917, civilian Councils of Defense were set up all over the country to coordinate the war effort. In a number of Oklahoma counties, these organizations resorted to extra-legal methods to enforce what they regarded as patriotic attitudes. These self-appointed defenders of the American way of life candidly and publicly proclaimed their tactics of intimidation: "A few men convicted in Federal Courts, a few fined, a few held up to the ridicule of their neighbors, and perhaps a few shot, would mean the absolute stamping out of pro-Germanism in Oklahoma."[14] Inspired by such sentiments, there occurred incidents of violence, coercion, and humiliation directed against German-language groups around the state.

To many of the superpatriots of those days, the Mennonites seemed to pose a double menace: they spoke German and they opposed military conscription. Consequently, the Washita County Council of Defense prohibited the use of the German language in their churches, generally intimidated them, and drafted their sons into the army regardless of their religious scruples. Jacob's eldest son was conscripted; his nephew, John Klaassen, was sentenced to twenty-five years' imprisonment for his refusal to bear arms. He died at Leavenworth in 1918. When the boy's body was sent home for burial, his father, Michael Klaassen, created a local scandal by replacing his uniform with civilian clothes prior to interment. America had turned inhospitable.

Reluctantly and bitterly, Jacob chose to emigrate again before his other sons could be drafted. Upon parting from his church and loved ones, he could not contain his tears: "Had I not lived the most beautiful part of my life on this little piece of ground? I had lived there with my dear wife and growing children. I had worked, prayed, and fought there, . . . had many glad and joyous hours there, and had also struggled through the deepest sorrow."[15] After twenty-four years of pioneering in Oklahoma, Jacob and his sons moved to Canada. He remained on his farm in Saskatchewan until his death in 1948.

Perhaps half the membership of Klaassen's Herold Church joined him in his migration to Canada in the fall of 1918. But many others remained, for the Mennonite community of Corn was numerous and prosperous. By the year of statehood they had founded eight churches in Washita County alone, and the Mennonite Brethren had their own Bible Academy at Corn. The Mennonites of the Washita Valley continued to exert a powerful influence in Oklahoma.

They formed only a part of the Russian-German population of the area, however. Among the 736 Russian-born Germans who lived there in 1910, there were a number of other denominations whose experiences and heritage were as colorful as that of the Mennonites. One settlement, for example, developed around the Zion Congregational Church, six miles southeast of Weatherford. It consisted primarily of immigrants from the neighboring Volga colonies of Norka, Frank, and Kolb, who had settled originally in Adams County, Nebraska, in 1879. Among those prominent in this community were the Adler, Amen, Hamburger, Koch, Sauer, and Traudt families. Germans from Russia also participated in the formation of the German Baptist Church about two miles east of Bessie in 1895.[16]

Bessie was also the focus of two of the best known early Lutheran churches in the Washita region. A group of Germans from Beresina, in Russian Bessarabia—including the Belter, Ressler, and Stehr families—came to Oklahoma by way of North Dakota and settled the area northwest of Bessie before the turn of the century. Under the leadership of Jacob Ressler, this community built its own church of native stone. While the women dressed rocks they found on the banks of a nearby creek, the men hauled them to the site and set them in place. Clay from the creek served both as mortar for the walls as well as plaster to smooth the interior. The ceiling and walls they then decorated with floral designs and verses from the Bible. For a total cost of $75, these pioneers built their own house of worship, the Zion Lutheran Church. Most people called it the Rock Church, however, a name by which it is yet known, though today it stands in ruins. Still an imposing structure about one-half mile east of Bessie is the Peace American Lutheran Church. Its founders came down from Lehigh, Kansas, to homestead the area in 1892 and 1893. Under the leadership of Gottlieb Goeringer, who had been a schoolmaster in Russia, they established this church as the focal point of their community. Among its early parishioners were the Bessler, Bredy, Ernst, Jaworsky, Kolb, Mueller, Proskey, Steigman, and Weil families, all of whom had come from the town of Kamenka, on the east bank of the Dniester River in Russian Podolia. They had been settled there by Prince Ludwig zu Sayn und Wittgenstein (1768–1842), one of the Czar's German generals who had distinguished himself as the commander of the Russian armies that defeated Napoleon in 1813. As a reward for his services, the Czar presented Kamenka to Wittgenstein, who developed it agriculturally, built factories and shops, and imported German peasants and craftsmen to make it productive. His estate subsequently became a resort for the Russian aristocracy and their artistic protégés. Even today there are in Bessie family traditions and stories in which such greats as Alexander Pushkin, Franz Liszt, and Anton Rubinstein figure prominently.[17]

To the south of Washita County, the Germans from Russia extended their settlements into the foothills of the Wichita Mountains when the Comanche, Kiowa, and Apache lands were opened by lottery in 1901. Already in 1894, the Mennonite Brethren had established a mission to the Comanches at Post Oak, near Indiahoma in Comanche County. This denomination had originated in the Ukraine in 1860 when a small group of pietistic leaders broke away from the main body of Mennonites in order to enforce more rigorous standards of conduct and give greater emphasis to prayer and Bible study. The migration to the United States drew extensively from the Mennonite Brethren, and they soon organized a strong American church with an emphasis upon missionary activity. The first two missionaries at the Post Oak station, Henry Kohfeld and Abraham J. Becker, were both born in Russia.

The Reverend Henry Kohfeld approached Quanah Parker, Chief of the Comanches, for permission to build a mission on their reservation about twenty miles west of Fort Sill in 1894. Though the chief was reluctant at first, one of his wives interceded on behalf of the

The wedding picture of Edward and Rosina Steigman, Bessie, Oklahoma, 1910. The Steigmans originally came from Kamenka, Podolia. Courtesy of Ray D. Lau.

missionary, and Parker blazed the trunk of a post oak tree to mark the site of the proposed mission. After obtaining a grant of land to support the station, Kohfeld set about constructing the necessary buildings and clearing the land.

To aid him in this endeavor, he invited twenty-three-year-old Abraham J. Becker down from Isabella, near Fairview. Born in 1872 at the Mennonite village of Wohldemfürst in the Russian Caucasus, young Becker was the son of one of the founders of the Mennonite Brethren denomination. His father moved the family to Kansas when Abraham was a child and subsequently to Oklahoma Territory. Becker became avidly interested in the life of the Comanche people and after completing a course of study at McPherson College, Kansas, he married and joined Kohfeld as a full-time missionary at Post Oak in 1901.

Becker and his wife devoted their lives to this mission. The missionary became Quanah Parker's dearest and most trusted friend, and when the old chief died in 1911, Becker officiated at his funeral.

Subsequently, the Beckers began working among the Mexican laborers who had settled in nearby Lawton. In 1935 he established a mission for them which later became the Lawton View Mennonite Brethren Church. Until his death in 1942 Becker was among the most prominent religious leaders in Comanche County. One of his six children was William J. Becker, a distinguished linguist and long-time head of the Language Arts Department at Cameron State University. From the distant Kuban River of the Russian Caucasus, the Becker family thus brought their unique talents and dedication to southwest Oklahoma.[18]

Most of the Russian Germans who came to this area settled farther to the northwest, however, between Gotebo and Hobart in Kiowa County. The former, once a thriving town of nearly one thousand inhabitants, boasted three Mennonite churches and a school in 1910. There were also the Salem Baptist Church west of Gotebo, which was attended by a number of Russian-German families, and a Lutheran church in the town itself. Though others were scattered elsewhere in the Wichita Mountain area, Gotebo remained the heart of this settlement. Of the 234 Russian-born Germans in Kiowa County in 1910, more than half lived in the Gotebo vicinity.[19]

Pioneering was hard in southwestern Oklahoma; it was difficult for a man to give up all he had worked for in the old country and begin anew from nothing. Such was the case of John Jacob Laufer. He had grown up in the city of Saratov on the Volga, where he worked as a coachman on the estate of the Schmidt family, Russian Germans who had grown rich in the flour milling and textile trades. Here Laufer met his future bride, Barbara Weber, when she came up from the German colony of Messer to serve as a lady's maid in the Schmidt household. The young couple were no sooner engaged, however, than John was drafted for five years' service in the army.

It turned out to be a profitable experience. The young man showed intelligence and managerial ability and earned promotions to positions of considerable responsibility. Upon his return to Saratov and his marriage in 1896, there was little thought of returning to the humble occupation of coachman; John became instead a flour salesman for the Schmidt Brothers firm. By 1902 he was secretary for a flour mill and had a growing family of four children.

But conditions in Russia were tense and threatening. Barbara's parents had long since left the Volga for Oklahoma, so the young couple decided to join them in the spring of 1903. By this time transatlantic crossings had become fairly safe and convenient, and

The John Jacob Laufer family with a neighbor (upper left). This portrait was taken shortly before the family left Saratov for Kiowa County, Oklahoma. Courtesy of Miss Ottilia Laufer.

John could afford comfortable accommodations for his family. They traveled by German liner from Bremen to New York, and on June 15, 1903, Barbara was joyfully reunited with her family near Okeene. Her husband, however, was faced with the challenge of beginning all over again in a new and unfamiliar land.

Speaking no English and inexperienced at farming, the young businessman found only menial jobs open to him. He first eked out a living as a farm laborer and then moved his family to Kansas City where he obtained work as a railroad carriage cleaner by day and a shoe cobbler by night. After more than a year of this, the Laufers made their way back to Oklahoma and eventually settled on a quarter section about six miles west of Gotebo, where John turned to farming.

It was a toilsome existence — a far cry from the rather comfortable life the Laufers had known in Russia. John knew little about farming, and there were many difficult and costly lessons to be learned. Barbara not only had to join her husband in the field but also care for her growing brood of eight children. Her first home was a 12-foot by 16-foot shack; she and John dug their own well. Cotton growing required backbreaking labor by the whole family from summer until

Christmas, often with scant return. Sometimes the couple wondered why they had ever left Russia. But slowly, by dint of enormous effort, the Laufers succeeded as an American farm family. While hailstorms and drought drove others from the land, they held on and gradually began to prosper. By 1909 they could enlarge their home; a few years later, John bought his own threshing equipment. One year a kerosene stove was added, an automobile the next. Little by little, life became more comfortable. On this farm the Laufers lived for forty years, pioneers from Russia on southwestern Oklahoma soil.[20]

Chapter 3

FROM THE CIMARRON
TO NO MAN'S LAND

As the Cimarron winds through Major, Blaine, and Kingfisher counties, a number of its tributary streams have cut channels through the alluvial plains of its south bank. Upon the terraces between these creeks, hundreds of Germans from Russia found good soil for wheat cultivation in the 1890s. Served principally today by Fairview and Okeene, this zone stretches about thirty-five miles along the river, from Orienta to Loyal. By 1910, 858 Russian-born Germans lived there. Some had settled western Kingfisher and Blaine counties with the opening of 1892, but most had moved into Major County after the Cherokee Outlet Run the following year. As elsewhere, their churches provided the centers of community life and the nodes around which these settlements developed.

Mennonites came early to the area. One of their first establishments, the General Conference Mennonite Church at Geary, was a direct consequence of Indian missionary activity. With the extinction of tribal title to the Cheyenne-Arapaho lands in 1892, many Indians chose individual allotments along the North Canadian River. The Reverend Jacob S. Krehbiel decided to take the church to them. Consequently, he made the Run of 1892, obtained land about four miles north of the present site of Geary, and built a mission chapel there. When Geary was founded in 1898, the church was moved into the town. A number of Germans from Russia participated in the founding of this community.[1]

Other churches in the region affiliated with the Mennonite Brethren denomination. In 1892 immigrants from Russia founded the Ebenfeld Mennonite Brethren Church southwest of Okeene; others formed a church at Cooper, near Hitchcock, a year later. Then, with the opening of the Cherokee Outlet, settlers from the

Molotschna colonies of the Ukraine established two communities on either side of present-day Fairview: North Hopefield and South Hopefield. By 1895 both settlements had built sod churches. Subsequently replaced by more permanent structures, the two congregations remained separate until consolidated into the Fairview Mennonite Brethren Church in 1951.[2]

Perhaps the most prominent and popular of the early Mennonite Brethren leaders in the Fairview area was the Reverend Martin M. Just (1866–1919). His grandparents had migrated from Grenzdorf, near Danzig, to the Ukraine in 1847. The Just family was Lutheran by faith and quite prosperous, but its serenity and stability were disturbed by the religious ferment occasioned by the propagation of the new Mennonite Brethren doctrine after 1860. Martin, the eldest son of the family, found the spirit of the new creed much to his liking, and both he and his wife were baptized as Mennonite Brethren in 1873. This apostasy from the faith of their fathers provoked a breach within the family, and Martin Just moved away from his home village. The difficulty of finding available land and the imposition of military conscription also persuaded Just and his wife to abandon Alexandertal on the Molotschna for America in 1880.

By this time, their family consisted of five children; Martin M. Just, at fourteen, was the eldest. After a journey by way of Bremen and New York, the family set up housekeeping on a farm near Aulne, Marion County, Kansas. Here young Martin grew to manhood; as the eldest boy, he was already expected to do a man's work. Besides, his father, a jolly, gentle man, was already very stout, quickly ran out of breath, and needed his help. Young Martin coupled his capacity for hard work as a farm hand with a fascination for books and learning. Though he had but a rudimentary education, he read voraciously every book that came his way. He also served as family secretary, accountant, and purchasing agent, which spared his father the task of learning English.

At age twenty-one Martin M. Just married Anna Schapansky who lived on a nearby farm. He first supported his bride by working in a railroad section gang—at eleven cents per hour—but soon managed to rent a farm. Like so many others, Martin and his young family moved from place to place during the early years of his marriage, and he found additional jobs whenever he could. By 1893 he had accumulated enough to buy an eighty-acre place in Marion County and joyfully moved his wife and four daughters into the first home of their very own. The following year brought heartbreak, however, as Martin lost both his wife and a newborn son in death. It almost crushed him.

But already the young man was deeply involved in the religious life of the community: it now became the center of his existence. This, in addition to the responsibility he felt for his daughters, provided the resolution necessary for a new start. He remarried and in 1895 moved to the Cherokee Outlet. Martin bought a quarter section in the Isabella community, southeast of present-day Fairview, for $200 and began pioneer life anew in a sod house. In those days, the nearest source of supplies was the railhead at Enid, a three-day trip by wagon, assuming that the Cimarron could be forded without difficulty. On this farm, Just and his wife reared seven daughters.

For the remainder of his life, Martin M. Just dedicated himself to the South Hopefield Mennonite Brethren church. The congregation chose him as their minister, a post he occupied for twenty-two years. He was also an important figure in the General Conference of the church and became prominent throughout Kansas and Oklahoma in this role. Just was not only a dedicated servant of the faith; he was a singularly genial and warmhearted man as well. When

The Reverend Martin M. Just of Fairview, Oklahoma, 1918. Courtesy of Mrs. Lea Wahl.

he died in 1919, the tributes to his memory were impressive and sincere.[3]

While the Mennonite Brethren were most numerous in the Fairview area, there was still a great deal of religious diversity among the Germans from Russia. They established a Mennonite Church of God in Christ and a General Conference Mennonite Church in the vicinity. German Baptist churches were founded at Kiel (Loyal), Kingfisher, and Okeene, where parishes of the German Evangelical Synod of North America were also located. Many immigrants from Russia became Seventh-Day Adventists. American in origin, the Adventists had sent missionaries to Russia in the 1880s, where they found an eager reception among the German colonists. Already the faith had struck deep roots in Marion County, Kansas. Russian-German settlers from that area founded churches between the Cimarron and North Canadian at Cooper, Fairview, Hitchcock, Okeene, Omega, and Southard. Still other immigrants joined the various Lutheran churches in the region [4]

Though thousands of Russian-German Catholics had settled in Kansas, only a handful found their way to Oklahoma. A good example of their experience is provided by John J. Farhar, the blacksmith of Okeene. He came from the Catholic colony of Semenovka, which had been founded by Hessian immigrants about twenty miles west of the Volga in 1767. Born in 1883, Farhar worked as a blacksmith's apprentice during his youth. At age twenty-one he was drafted for four years' service in the Russian Army just in time for the Russo-Japanese War. Returning to his home town, the young blacksmith married Anna M. Gette in 1908.

In the meantime, his old employer, Fred Winters, had come to America and settled at Okeene. Shortly after their marriage, John and Anna Farhar received two steamship tickets from Winters. Traveling by way of Germany and Galveston, the couple arrived at Okeene on March 17, 1909. After working for Winters for a time, Farhar opened his own shop. By 1921 he was able to build the home in which he and his wife would rear fourteen children. They were all members of St. Anthony of Padua Church, and the children all attended St. Mary's School. Mrs. Farhar died in 1971; John Farhar, a veteran of the Russo-Japanese War, still lives in Okeene.[5]

If denominational diversity distinguished the Russian-Germans of the Cimarron Valley from each other, they shared many more things in common. In terms of origin, the vast majority came either from the Evangelical colonies of the Volga or the Mennonite villages

Mr. John J. Farhar of Okeene, Oklahoma. Courtesy of Joseph Farhar.

on the Molotschna. About 85 percent had lived previously in or near Marion County, Kansas, before moving to Oklahoma Territory. For the most part, they consisted of young parents with growing families, and all but a few shared one overriding condition: poverty. This was what made free land in Oklahoma attractive to them despite the high cost it exacted in privation and hard work.

This poverty exacerbated the hardships, dangers, and physical discomfort which were a normal and expected part of pioneering. Virtually all of them made their first homes in houses of sod, or more frequently, dugouts. Especially for the Russian-German housewife, reared as she was in a tradition of immaculate cleanliness, consider-able ingenuity was required to render one of these hovels habitable. Mrs. Lena Wichert, for instance, plastered the interior of her sod house northwest of Fairview with clay she dug and mixed herself. Then she used laundry bluing to paint a grape arbor design around the interior walls. It was beautiful—until it rained, and the fragile fresco washed down the sides.[6]

For most people, however, the *lack* of rain created major problems. Even the very elements seemed to conspire to break the spirit of the first pioneers. The period of settlement coincided with a long dry cycle. Precipitation was only about one-half its normal level, and only in 1897 was the drought broken. If, through arduous labor and exceptionally good luck, a little wheat or cotton was raised, a two- or three-days' journey was required to market the product. Men, women, and children simply had to work unceasingly if the family were to survive.

And children there were in abundance, given the numerous offspring characteristic of the Germans from Russia. Families of more than a dozen were quite common. John Jantzen and his wife, who homesteaded southeast of Okeene, packed sixteen children into a three-room house. George Peter Nusz, of Dobrinka on the Volga, raised fourteen children on his farm near Isabella. Peter and Katherine Lorenz supported twelve offspring on their place in the Cooper vicinity. These were the norm. Many hands were needed to do the work, and in some parts of Russia land had been allocated in proportion to the size of the family. Besides, the ravages of disease—diphtheria, typhoid, pneumonia—especially among the very young, made a high birth rate a necessity for survival.[7]

Fires, farm accidents, and other disasters took a similar toll. One family was wiped out when in their ignorance of English they mistook gasoline for kerosene. Two members of the Koop family and a neighbor were asphyxiated at the bottom of a well they were digging near Fairview in 1893. One memorable prairie fire is still imprinted upon the consciousness of some of the Mennonites near Geary, though it occurred more than eighty years ago. As they were practicing their Christmas program at the church in 1894, someone noticed a column of smoke rising from the Red Hills to the northwest. The wind suddenly shifted to the north, and a freezing gale blew the fire across the tinder-dry prairie toward the settlement. All rushed home, filled barrels and buckets with water, grabbed feed sacks, and dashed to the fire line. Within half an hour, the flames had raced seven miles, and it was ten o'clock that night before the exhausted settlers could contain them. Fortunately, no lives were lost. By the time the firefighters returned home, the cold wind had frozen stiff the wet sacks used to beat out the fire.[8]

As though such perils and hardships were not sufficient to test the mettle of the Cimarron pioneers, a plague of outlaws descended upon them in the mid-nineties to contribute another element of insecurity to their already marginal existence. The two most notorious of these desperadoes were Zip Wyatt (alias Dick Yeager) and Ike

Douglas Hale

Black. A posse exterminated the pair in the summer of 1895, but not before they had acquired an aura of romance and glamour sufficient to inspire emulators among the local hoodlum element. Various would-be badmen made sport of terrorizing the newcomers from Russia—shooting up a farm house here and stealing a horse there—as their whim dictated.[9]

One such encounter involved the family of Jacob J. Bierig, who came from the Evangelical colony of Bauer, twenty-five miles west of the Volga. In 1892, his entire family immigrated to the United States, settled temporarily in Durham, Kansas, and made the run into the Cherokee Outlet the following year. Jacob, his wife, and three children homesteaded a place about two miles east of Isabella, in what would become Major County. Here Jacob built a two-story log house for his family and set up a sod blacksmith shop.

One bitterly cold afternoon in January, 1896, a local man called at Jacob's shop to have his horse shod. He owed but fifty cents for the job, but he gave Bierig a ten-dollar bill. The blacksmith sent his son, Little Jake, into the house to fetch change for his customer. The nine-year-old boy took the tobacco sack in which their money was kept from its hiding place in the baby's cradle and brought it to his father. As Bierig handed him his change, the caller observed that the sack was full of bills. Indeed, Jacob Bierig had been saving for a year to buy a team of horses. Later that day, he paid this debt, leaving but $2.04 in the family treasury.

Shortly after dark that evening, the customer of the afternoon returned to the Bierig farm with two confederates. While he remained outside, his partners in crime gained entry to the house at the point of a gun and demanded all of Jacob's money. Unresisting, the father sent his son to fetch the tobacco sack, and Little Jake handed over the $2.04 which it contained. The two men grabbed the money and dashed out the door. They would have left the family unscathed, but Little Jake recognized the afternoon caller through a window and called out his name. Infuriated, one of his partners aimed his gun through the half-opened door and shot the boy in the head. The robbers then rode off to squander their hard-won loot at a pie supper in Isabella.

The bullet entered the child's left cheek below the temple, ranged downward, and shattered the right jaw as it exited. The victim lay untreated until three o'clock the following morning, until his father and uncle could drive through driving sleet the twelve miles to Ringwood and back with a doctor. The physician syringed out the wound with a carbolic acid solution and drew a silk handkerchief through the boy's face to remove the shattered bone.

The sheriff of old Woods County arrested the assailants shortly thereafter and brought them to Alva for trial. But the three hoodlums obtained the services of a clever and prominent lawyer who through various stratagems got the trial delayed until October, 1897, almost two years after the crime. The prosecution was further handicapped because Jacob Bierig and his wife spoke no English. The only witness to the crime who could testify directly to the court was Little Jake himself, and he was only eleven years old. In the end, the jury acquitted the three robbers.[10]

Still the story has a happy ending. Though he lost the sight of his left eye, Little Jake survived his ordeal quite nicely, grew up, married, and raised six children. He died in 1971 at the age of 85. The Germans from Russia were a hardy people.

All the hardihood they could muster would be necessary to endure the harsh climatic conditions of the Cherokee Outlet to the north and west. Like the Bierigs, hundreds of Russian Germans moved into its six million acres following the opening of 1893. The more desirable sections to the east were snapped up overnight. Those in the west were left unoccupied for almost a decade, since most potential settlers perceived correctly that the land was too arid for conventional farming. As late as 1900 only 31 percent of the western sections had been claimed.[11] Thus the Germans from Russia generally established their communities in the Outlet from east to west, forming eight major settlements. Though they were rural communities for the most part, they may be identified with the following towns: Medford and Deer Creek in Grant County; Enid; the Goltry-Lahoma-Meno area; Cherokee in Alfalfa County; Coy in north-western Woods County; Woodward; and Shattuck.

Shortly after the Run of 1893, a number of Mennonites from the area of Moundridge and Halstead, Kansas, settled in the Deer Creek vicinity. Some of the first leaders of this community had come from Germany or from older Mennonite centers in the East. But there were also many Germans from Russia among them, including the Dirksen, Fast, and Peters families. In the spring of 1898, the town of Deer Creek was laid out almost adjoining the farms of the Mennonite homesteaders. The present Deer Creek Mennonite Church was formally organized the following year.[12]

Medford became a center for both Mennonite Brethren and

General Conference Mennonites from Russia. As was often the case, both churches were associated with outstanding leaders during their early days. Mennonite Brethren families from Lehigh, Kansas, began settlement of the Medford area in the spring of 1894, led by Johann J. Wiens and David Harms. Others soon joined them, including J. F. Harms (1855–1945), editor of the *Zionsbote*, the official organ of the church. Medford thus became the heart of the Mennonite Brethren movement during Harm's residence there.

He was a native of Kleefeld, a village on the Molotschna River in South Russia, where he had been a teacher in the colonies until he brought his family to Minnesota in 1878. Ever a wanderer, Harms next moved to Indiana to begin his career as an editor. In 1884, with his assumption of the editorship of the *Zionsbote* ("Messenger of Zion"), he became one of the most influential leaders of his church. After residence in Hillsboro, Kansas, for some years, Harms moved to a farm about two and one-half miles north of Medford in 1899 and published his journal here for the next seven years. Through the pages of the *Zionsbote,* Mennonite Brethren around the world maintained contact with each other and followed developments of concern to their church. Because of his wife's ill health, however, Harms moved to Canada in 1906, and the Mennonite Brethren congregation of Medford was dissolved several years later. Harms lived on to the age of ninety, continued his active leadership in the church, and became well known for his relief work in Russia during the Great Famine of 1921.[13]

The present General Conference Mennonite Church of Medford was originally organized in 1897 northeast of the town. Its founder and first minister, Heinrich J. Gaede (1861–1932), would serve the church for nineteen years. His forebears had migrated from Thorn, West Prussia, to the Ukraine at the beginning of the nineteenth century, and Gaede was born in the Molotschna village of Mariawohl. Orphaned at the age of eight, young Gaede was reared by a foster family who brought him to Lehigh, Kansas, as a youth. He learned the trade of carpenter and at the age of twenty-two married Maria Epp. The couple had been married for almost a decade and had six children when the opening of the Cherokee Outlet gave Gaede a chance to acquire his own farm.

In 1895 Gaede moved his family into the Medford area and built a sod house near the bank of a creek. The first high water washed away their dwelling and most of their belongings; for a time the family found refuge in an empty store building at Medford.

Little by little, however, Gaede began to accumulate enough to provide his brood a decent living. He bought an improved farm three miles from town. He also helped organize the Mennonite Church, and though without any formal ministerial training, was chosen as its first pastor. Eight of the Gaede children survived to adulthood and earned considerable local renown for their musical talents. In 1916 the family moved to Arizona and subsequently to California, where Gaede continued to serve as a pastor. The church and community he did so much to build still flourish in Medford.[14]

In the early settlement of the Enid area, both Mennonite Brethren and Lutherans were important. In 1874 about thirty-five Brethren families emigrated from the Molotschna Valley to the Henderson, Nebraska, vicinity. Because of severe drought conditions, however, a number of these people looked elsewhere for a new start. In 1893, a few of these Brethren made the run into the Cherokee Outlet. Others followed and bought relinquishments in the area to the north of the new town of Enid. They proceeded immediately to organize their religious life, worshipping first in private homes and a nearby schoolhouse. Under the leadership of Klaas Penner and Peter Regier, thirty charter members formally founded a church in 1897. Their work lives on in the Enid Mennonite Brethren Church. A few miles to the northeast stands the present Immanuel Lutheran Church at Breckinridge. It became the center of a settlement of Germans from the Volga who came into the area a few years later.[15]

West of Enid, bounded roughly by the villages of Ringwood, Goltry, and Lahoma, a large concentration of Germans from Russia developed shortly after the opening of the Cherokee Outlet. By 1910, 205 Russian-born Germans lived in the area. Most were Mennonites, and the village of Meno, named after the founder of the faith, lies at the heart of this enclave. In 1895, seven years before the town itself was organized, a group of immigrants led by Benjamin D. Jantz and Johann Ratzlaff established the New Hopedale Mennonite Church. In time it became the largest General Conference church in Oklahoma and gave rise to the Oklahoma Bible Academy, a Mennonite secondary school chartered in 1911. Other churches served as the nuclei around which additional Russian-German communities formed near Lahoma, Ringwood, and Goltry.[16]

About thirty miles to the northwest, a smaller enclave of Germans from Russia developed between Cherokee and Burlington in Alfalfa County. The heart of this community was the village of Ingersoll, near the Salt Fork of the Arkansas. Virtually all of these immigrants

42

had originated in the three colonies of Messer, Kutter, or Moor, which lay within eight miles of each other on the Hill Side of the Volga. Unlike most of those who came to Oklahoma, these people had settled first in Barton and Rush counties of western Kansas rather than the Marion County area. While the majority had followed the Evangelical faith in Russia, they became Baptists in America. Though a few affiliated with the Lutherans, most were members of the Bethel Baptist Church of Ingersoll, the services of which were held in German.[17]

Typical in many ways of the experiences of these immigrants has been the life of Henry Weber of Cherokee. He is the descendent of German pioneers from Böges, near Eisenach in Thuringia, who settled the Volga colony of Messer shortly after it was founded in 1766. Here his family remained for more than a century as the place grew into a sizable town of about 5,000 inhabitants. Still it retained its nuclear village form: the homes of its residents were clustered around a central thoroughfare, while the farm lands lay around the periphery of the town. The farmers did not own the land individually; it was vested in the community as a whole. Every ten years the village

Threshing barley by hand at Messer Colony, Volga. Courtesy of American Historical Society of Germans from Russia.

council would reapportion the land among the inhabitants according to the number of males in each family.

Messer was a prosperous and pleasant place. It had a splendid old wooden church with an onion dome and a separate bell tower. The colonists were largely self-sufficient, raising wheat, rye, barley, and oats, as well as fruits and vegetables. The town had four flour mills of its own, and few necessities had to be bought outside. There was little reason for most of the inhabitants to develop contacts with the Russian population of the surrounding countryside. The only Russian who actually lived in Messer itself was the local magistrate.

Such was the colony when Henry Weber was born there in 1886, one of six children. His father farmed about eighty acres of land, and each child had his designated chores to perform. By the time he was seven, Henry was herding horses at night on the lonely steppe. Every child learned a trade as well. While other members of the family turned to harness making or learned the skills of the wheelwright, Henry, appropriately enough considering his surname, became a weaver. He obtained yarn from a local merchant and spent the long Russian winters at his loom. It took him about three weeks to weave a 160-yard bolt of cotton cloth, for which he would receive the equivalent of $14.40 for his labor. Not all his time was spent working, however, for Henry attended the local school from the time he was six until the age of fourteen and proved an able student.

As Henry approached his eighteenth birthday and liability for conscription into the Russian Army, his father decided that the time had come to emigrate to America. He had toyed with the idea ever since 1874, when the Germans lost their military exemption, and already a number of his relatives had left Messer and had settled in Oklahoma. To delay the step much longer would be to subject his son to at least four years of military service. Consequently, the Weber family sold all their possessions and set out for the United States in November, 1903.

Taking only their clothing and a large basket of food, they traveled by rail to Bremen. There were no dining facilities on ordinary Russian trains, but huge samovars stood in the stations, from which passengers could draw hot water for the preparation of meals. At one stop, Henry and two other passengers left their car to fetch hot water, and the train started up without them. He still recalls the breathless race down the tracks after the train: "All our papers and money were with our parents, and we would have been in real trouble if we had missed it. But we caught it, and didn't spill any of the water."

At Bremen the family boarded the *Breslau,* a German liner, and after a fairly pleasant crossing of twelve days, arrived in New York. They went through immigration formalities without leaving the ship and then continued on to Galveston, arriving on Henry's birthday, January 11, 1904. From there they traveled by train to Isabella, in Major County, where Henry's uncle met the family. The cost of the entire trip was less than $100 per person.

Henry's father and mother bought a farm southeast of Okeene, and their son lived there for four years. At age twenty-one he moved to the Ingersoll vicinity to begin farming on his own. Though he had belonged to the Reformed Church in Russia, he was baptized into the Bethel Baptist Church of Ingersoll. He served this church as Sunday School Superintendent for fourteen years and as Secretary for twenty-one more. Here Henry Weber married and raised his family. He still resides in nearby Cherokee, cheerfully willing and able to describe in detail life in turn-of-the-century Russia for the interested listener.[18]

Proceeding westward into Woods County, we find that two rural communities of Russian Germans were in evidence at the time of statehood. The smaller of the two lay between Avard and Alva and included the Brickman and Heise families. In the extreme north-western corner of Woods County, near Coy, a second community developed. Some of these were Mennonite veterans of the Great Trek through Central Asia. A group of Lutherans lived nearby; they joined their coreligionists across the Cimarron in Harper County to form the Zion Lutheran Church near Charleston in 1903. Among its parishioners were the Krenz, Martin, Ring, Uhrig, Weimer, and Yauk families. Most of these people had come originally from the Volga colonies and settled the Territory between 1901 and 1904.[19]

One of these pioneer families was that of David Martin. He came from the Evangelical colony of Holstein, founded on the Hill Side of the Volga in 1765. David's uncle, John Krenz, had left Holstein in 1885 and settled at Osage City, Kansas, where he became a coal miner. At the age of twenty-six, David decided to join his uncle and in September, 1899, departed Holstein with his wife Maria and their four-year-old son. At Osage City, David found a job in a road gang at a dollar a day. Since he had been earning only about $25 per year as a farm laborer in Russia, David felt quite prosperous, rejoiced at his good fortune, and began looking for new worlds to conquer.

In March, 1901, John Krenz and his nephew learned that free land was still available in the Cherokee Outlet. They traveled to

Woodward by train, found out where the vacant sections were located, and continued by horseback thirty miles or so to inspect the tracts recommended to them. Both Krenz and Martin home-steaded quarter sections about eight miles northeast of Buffalo. Since David did not have the required $14· filing fee, he raised the money by digging a well for a local farmer.

The following September the two men loaded their families and belongings aboard a railway car and moved them all to Ashland, Kansas, the railhead nearest their property but still twenty miles away. By this time, David and Maria had three small children, and there were also three children in the Krenz family. Martin and Krenz set up tents for the women and children at Ashland; they then proceeded by wagon to their claims to build homes. David dug several feet into a slope, added sod walls to the dugout, and completed the roof of his 14-foot by 24-foot dwelling with tarpaper, boards, and sod. Within three weeks, the two families had been moved into their new homes. With two other families, they were the only settlers in the area at first, though by the next summer homesteaders would occupy every quarter section. The little community of New Hope had been born.

Meanwhile, David faced the necessity of feeding his family. For $10 he bought a milk cow and acquired a dozen hens. From E. M. Best, a storekeeper at Brule, some eight miles away, he obtained credit for the winter and the assurance that Martin was "one Dutch-man that I will trust." To pay for all this, the young homesteader was forced to leave his wife and children alone on the prairie while he returned to Osage City to mine coal during the winter.

With her accustomed courageous serenity, Maria Martin met the challenge. Her nearest neighbors, the Krenz family, lived a mile away. She had to haul water a quarter of a mile from a spring and gather cow chips for fuel. All went well: the children remained healthy, and the winter was a relatively mild one. But because of the unusual weather there was a decreased demand for coal, and the mine at Osage City shut down in March, 1902, leaving her husband unemployed. At least he could return to his family. David rode a boxcar from Osage City to Wichita and then struck out overland by foot. It required about a week for him to cover the remaining 160 miles, stopping overnight at farmhouses along the way.

The spring looked promising to a man of Martin's habitual optimism. Maria and the children were well; the soil was moist and ready for planting. David spent his savings from Osage City on a sod

The David Martin family of New Hope Community, Harper County, where they settled in 1901. Courtesy of Godfrey Martin.

plow, a planter, and a team of horses and started a garden as well as ten acres of kaffir corn. By late summer his farm was well established, and his family was living almost exclusively on the produce of their own land—a situation of which both David and Maria were extremely proud. For seven years the growing family would occupy that original sod house until David could afford to build a proper two-story frame structure. Mrs. Martin raised her children in it: of the nine born to her, five survived the lethal diseases of childhood and grew to maturity. Both she and her husband remained on their farm until death: she in 1933, he in 1950.[20]

At the heart of the Russian-German community of Woodward County were three churches in the watershed of Turkey Creek, about five miles south of the hamlet of Tangier: a Lutheran, a Congregational, and a Seventh-Day Adventist. Together they counted in their membership 112 Germans who had been born in Russia. Among the Lutheran families was that of Ferdinand Meier from Shcherbakovka on the Volga. He had been born in 1862, settled first in Lehigh, Kansas, and came to Woodward County at the age of forty. Also Lutheran were members of the George Hohweiler family from the Volga colony of Stephan. His immigration to America had been delayed by army service until 1901. Johannes Weidner and his family were also Lutherans, but they came from Bessarabia. Among the Congregationalists in the community were the fifteen children of Gottfried Fiel. He had been born in Strassburg, on the Meadow Side of the Volga, and came to America in 1901. The Seventh-Day Adventist Church included the J. S. Becker family, who left Eigen-heim, Bessarabia, in 1892, settled first in Marion County, Kansas, and came to Woodward County in 1908.[21] The community has dispersed, all three churches have long since disappeared, but a number of these original families still reside in nearby Woodward or Fargo.

Twenty miles to the southwest, near Shattuck, Ellis County, Russian Germans established their most concentrated and homo-geneous settlement in the state. These people had homesteaded the Shattuck area in a surge of migration in 1901 and 1902; the next census showed that almost a thousand inhabitants were of first or second generation Russian-German stock. More than three-quarters of them had originally come from a handful of Evangelical towns on the west bank of the Volga—Stephan, Shcherbakovka, Dreispitz, and Holstein—all of which lay within ten miles of each other. Indeed, so many had come from the last-named place that they christened a new siding on the Santa Fe Railway after their hometown in Russia. Holstein, Oklahoma, later came to be called New Goodwin, however.

Most of the migrants had come into the area directly from Lehigh, Marion County, Kansas, and an unusually high proportion followed the Seventh-Day Adventist faith. Until 1900 this church formed the largest congregation in the then-thriving railroad town of Lehigh. But in the next two years the majority of the Lehigh Adventists migrated in a body to Ellis County to take advantage of the free land. Within a decade this county led the state of Oklahoma in Adventist membership, though considerable numbers of its Russian-German settlers affiliated with Baptist, Congregational, and Lutheran churches as well.

Most of the Lehigh immigrants were moved by special trains provided by the Santa Fe in the spring of 1901. They dismantled their wagons and tied them to the tops of the boxcars which con-tained their livestock. At milking time, the train would halt. The farmers would tend their animals and then bring pails of fresh milk back to their families in the passenger cars at the head of the train. Dogs and cats were brought along as well, but as an old settler put it, "one was smart: he turned around and went home." For the outlook in the new land was bleak indeed. A prairie fire had only recently swept the area, and all the passengers could see upon their arrival in Shattuck were endless miles of blackened earth stretching to the horizon.[22] But here they made their homes, and Shattuck today is still largely a Russian-German town; there are still more Ehrlichs and Herbers and Krafts and Schoenhals in the phone book than Smiths and Joneses.

Among those who participated in this exodus to the virgin lands of western Oklahoma was Dietrich Ehrlich. His ancestors had migrated from the Rhine to the Volga in 1764, where the family established itself at Shcherbakovka. The Ehrlichs became Baptists, and their nonconformity to the predominant Lutheranism of their community caused friction and hostility. Moreover, the Russification policies of the government intensified their discontent. Various members of the family chose the path of emigration, among them Dietrich, who at the age of twenty-four joined his parents in the American journey in 1891.

The family settled near Lehigh, where Dietrich's father took up his old trade as a tanner. The son, however, was forced to take odd jobs at low pay wherever they might be found. Dietrich married, five children were born, but the young man seemed as far from acquiring property and security for his family as he had ever been. In April, 1901, opportunity beckoned when the railroad offered to provide transportation to families who were willing to settle the Shattuck area. Dietrich seized the chance, homesteaded a quarter section about five miles south of Shattuck, dug a well, and built a crude lean-to to shelter his family.

Ehrlich began by planting broomcorn, milo, and maize, which were cut by hand and threshed by the hooves of horses in the ancient manner. Farm machinery was simply too expensive for the family to afford. Indeed, Ehrlich was unable to sustain his family by farming alone; he supplemented his income by building track for the railroad at two dollars per day. It was only after eleven years of arduous labor that he was able to build his family a proper house.

Slowly, however, life became more comfortable. Dietrich bought his first car in 1916; prosperous years permitted him to expand his holdings to an entire section during the 1920s. And there was a surprisingly active social life centering on the Seventh-Day Adventist Church less than a mile from the Ehrlich farm. Dietrich himself had helped organize the church shortly after his arrival in Oklahoma, and in many ways it remained the center of his existence. At the age of sixty-nine, the old farmer retired and turned over his holdings to his two sons. Ten years later he died.[23]

It was typical of the Germans from Russia to send two or three family members ahead into the new country to prepare the way and help earn passage for the family as a whole. Equally characteristic was their strong sense of family solidarity. More often than not, they remained together and settled adjacent lands despite all the vicissitudes of immigration and pioneering. The experience of the Johannes Georg Schoenhals family illustrates both these points.

Johannes Schoenhals, a cobbler and cabinet maker, was well over fifty and comfortably established in the colony of Stephan. In 1891, however, his two elder sons were threatened with conscription and therefore decided to leave Russia for good. In order to keep the family together, the father was reluctantly persuaded to abandon farm, home, tools, and livestock, and join the emigration. Since he had a wife and seven children, the money for such a monumental undertaking was hard to come by, so the two elder sons went ahead first, settled near an uncle at Lehigh, and saved their money. With their aid, the remainder of the family followed in 1893. One by one, sons and daughters took wives and husbands, but the Schoenhals family stayed together. Once again it was the sons who pushed ahead into the new land of Oklahoma: in March of 1901 George and Fred Schoenhals brought their young families into the Cherokee Outlet and homesteaded tracts south and west of Shattuck. The rest of the family soon followed suit, so that by 1903 Johannes, his wife Julia, and all seven children had settled within a few miles of each other. Today, of the 611 living descendents of Johannes and Julia Schoenhals, 208 reside within fifty miles of Shattuck.[24]

The Panhandle of Oklahoma was the home of three clearly defined communities of Germans from Russia by the year of statehood. The largest was in and around the town of Hooker, Texas County, where a total of 239 Russian-born Germans lived. The village of Balko in western Beaver County was the center of another smaller settlement, while twenty-five foreign-born Germans from Russia lived near what would become the hamlet of Turpin, to the north.

The land these people occupied had been settled only a short time before. "No Man's Land" became a part of Oklahoma Territory in 1890 and was opened to homesteaders. But a series of dry years rendered the treeless plains even less hospitable than usual, and the area at first attracted few settlers. Only after 1900, when the Free

Homes Act canceled all payment for homesteaded land and the Rock Island Railway completed its track from Liberal, Kansas, southwest into Texas, did a wave of homesteaders enter the region. The population of the Oklahoma Panhandle soared from 3,051 in 1900 to 32,433 in 1910.

Given the character of the land they chose to settle, these pioneers were a hardy lot indeed. In the words of Carl Rister, one of their chroniclers, "No sturdier, [more] resourceful people live on the American continent today than those of old No Man's Land. Like the hardy wind-blown and fiber toughened plant of the desert, they have survived every test to build a progressive culture." This tribute applied most fittingly to the Russian-German homesteaders of the Panhandle. Through hard work and persistence, they have helped make the region one of the most prosperous and progressive in the state.[25]

Many of these people who settled in the Hooker area were Mennonites. In 1904, the year in which the town itself was founded, a group of Mennonite Brethren from Buhler, Kansas, homesteaded land about eleven miles southeast of Hooker to form the hamlet of Adams. Nearby they established the Sharon Church some years later. Another Mennonite denomination represented in the Hooker vicinity was that of the Krimmer Mennonite Brethren, a small secessionist body which had been organized in the Crimea in 1869. The first Krimmer Brethren came to Kansas in 1874 and five years later they founded a church southwest of Inman, Kansas. From this congregation the Bethel Krimmer Church was organized near Hooker in 1907. It lasted only until 1919, however.[26]

Besides the Mennonites, there was a substantial Lutheran community near Hooker. Most of the Germans from Russia belonged to the Southside Lutheran Church, among them the Blehm, Fritzler, Herbel, Hofferber, Lundgrin, Winter, and Yauch families. All had come from the Hill Side of the Volga: the Blehms and Winters from Shcherbakovka; the Herbels, Hofferbers, and Lundgrins from Dreispitz; and the Fritzlers from Stephan. Other members of the Russian-German community belonged to the Seventh-Day Adventist Church in Hooker.[27]

Unlike this mixed denominational group near Hooker, those immigrants who settled across the line in Beaver County were virtually all Mennonites. Though Turpin was founded only in 1924 when a railroad built through the area, Mennonites from Russia had settled the vicinity as early as 1903. The first came from farms around

Buhler and Inman, Kansas. In 1907 they organized the Friedensfeld Mennonite Church about five miles northeast of the present site of Turpin. Among its early communicants were the Boese, Dirks, Epp, Fransen, Goertzen, and Zielke families. They also constructed a German school nearby which was used for many years.

About twenty miles south of Turpin, at Balko, a group of Mennonite Brethren established a church in 1906. This Balko community is particularly interesting as an example of how older communities in the emerging state provided the populations for the newer ones as settlement proceeded westward. It also illustrates in microcosm the intricate familial interrelationships among the Mennonite Brethren, though they be scattered far and wide. The founders of the Balko church were young couples just beginning their families. Almost all of them had come to the Panhandle directly from either the Fairview or Medford areas and were either close relatives or former parishioners of three prominent leaders of their church in Oklahoma: Jacob Kliewer, Martin M. Just, or J. F. Harms.

The first elected leader of the Balko church, for example, was Samuel L. Hodel, who had married Harms' daughter. He was born at Wohldemfürst in the Caucasus in 1877 and was brought to Kansas as a child. At twenty-two, Hodel married and moved to Medford where he worked on the farm of his father-in-law. Obtaining a homestead in Beaver County, the young farmer settled at Balko long enough to become the first pastor of its sod-house church in 1906. Within a year, however, the Hodels were off to Saskatchewan where they established a permanent home.

Another founding family, that of Abraham J. Neufeld, stayed in the Panhandle. Neufeld's parents brought him from the Molotschna colonies to Kansas in 1879. The boy grew up in the Hillsboro area and after his marriage moved to Blaine County, where he served as postmaster at Hitchcock until homesteading near Balko in 1905. Neufeld and his wife served the Balko Mennonite Brethren Church all their lives. Today, with a new building and a membership of 98, this church continues to flourish.[28]

Thus by 1907, the year of statehood, northwestern Oklahoma had a sizable population of Germans from Russia, almost all of whom lived in the rural communities of the region. Like other American farm families, their lives would be radically transformed by the economic and technological changes which occurred during the first three-quarters of the twentieth century: the decline of the family farm, the gradual urbanization of the population, the enormous social

Dave Klein, standing, upper left, a refugee from Dreispitz on the Volga to Shattuck, Oklahoma, 1922. Courtesy of Glenn Mueller.

and economic consequences of American global leadership since the Second World War, and the coming of the automobile and electronic mass communications. Their isolated, close-knit, and self-sufficient communities were thrown open to external influences; many of their towns and villages decayed as the young moved away to take advantage of greater opportunities. The Germans from Russia have been scattered far and wide. Yet in certain areas their heritage remains strong, one aspect of which is their unabashed love for this new land pioneered by their forefathers. To understand fully the singularly powerful strain of patriotism shared by these people, it would be well to reflect upon the fate of their kinsmen who remained behind in Russia.

Chapter 4

THOSE LEFT BEHIND

By the time of the First World War, most of the immigrants from Russia had lived in Oklahoma long enough to begin to enjoy the fruits of their labors. At last, most of them had comfortable if modest dwellings; a few began to buy their first automobiles. The promise of America was slowly becoming a reality. Tragically, the friends and loved ones whom they had left behind in Russia stood on the threshold of a far different future: the devastation of war, the destruction of revolution and civil war, the oppression of a monstrous tyranny, and the ultimate extinction of the society they had labored so hard to build. For an entire generation the Germans in Russia would know little else but violence, hunger, disease, and death.

In August, 1914, when the First World War broke out between Russia and Germany, the Russian government mobilized the German colonists along with the rest of the population. Touchingly loyal to the Czar, they deserved better than they received; some 250,000 German colonists fought in the Russian Army. Frequently their commanders callously used these troops as cannon fodder, and their casualties were unusually high. More seriously, wartime hysteria and hate directed against all things German singled out these inoffensive farmers, branded them "spies of the Kaiser," and inspired a campaign of officially sanctioned robbery and terror against the hapless foreigners.

When in 1915 the government sought a scapegoat for the disastrous military reverses which Russia had suffered, the German minority was ready at hand. Incited and encouraged by Russian officials, mobs vented their fury and frustration against German shops and farms. Government decrees forbade the colonists from speaking German and suppressed their newspapers. Other rulings expropriated the land which the Germans had so painfully pioneered, leaving hundreds of thousands of people destitute and homeless in the midst of war. The government ordered all Germans forceably evacuated from Volhynia, since the province lay too near the front lines. Police herded the old men, women, and children into cattle cars by night. These wretched victims were then hauled thousands of miles into Siberia or Central Asia to be interned in primitive camps on the deserted steppe. Some 120,000 people were thus driven from their farms. Unknown thousands perished; only about half would ever return to their homes.[1]

This program of liquidation was well under way when the February Revolution of 1917 halted it abruptly. The czarist regime collapsed under the weight of its own ineptitude, and a Provisional Government dedicated to liberalization and constitutional government succeeded to power. Though the war and its horrors continued, the German colonists saw a gleam of hope that they might be allowed to participate in the creation of a free Russia. The well-meaning Provisional Government promised a democratic system in which all the peoples of Russia could participate. For the first time, the Germans, who had consistently shunned and avoided political involvement, began to grope tentatively toward a role for themselves in the new Russia. But the events of the following October dashed all their hopes for freedom, reform, and recovery. The Bolsheviks seized power in the exhausted land, ended the war against Germany in March, 1918, and established a Communist dictatorship.

Under Lenin, the new Soviet government promised that all non-Russian minorities in the country would be accorded the right of "unrestricted development." The hopes so raised among the Germans proved but a cruel delusion. Instead of "unrestricted development," the German colonists found themselves subjected to the tender mercies of Communist commissars. And instead of peace, they, like the Russian peasants around them, were caught up in a disastrous Civil War in which they were victimized, plundered, and murdered by both sides for three years. The general state of anarchy gave rise to a reign of terror by ruthless brigands.

The armed bands of Nestor Makhno in the Ukraine were only the most conspicuous and notorious in their ferocity toward the German colonists. On November 10, 1919, for example, Makhno bandits trapped fourteen Mennonites in the basement of a house in Blumenort, on the Molotschna. The terrorists amused themselves by shooting at their victims for a while and then threw hand grenades among them. The pillagers killed six more men outside the house, raped every female in the village, and burned it to the ground. A few days later, Makhno raiders murdered 200 inhabitants and completely destroyed the German village of Münsterberg. The previous summer, a Red Army patrol caught 107 German farmers at a town meeting in Selze, near Odessa. The soldiers herded their unoffending victims to a graveyard, forced them to dig their own graves, and murdered them all. The list of Civil War atrocities is endless.[2]

During the Civil War all food, all grain, and all livestock which the impoverished colonists had managed to save were confiscated by the various armies. In one year the number of cattle in the Volga colonies dropped from 702,285 to 286,291. Owing to the confusion and the incompetence of the Communist officials, thousands of tons of supplies were wasted or allowed to rot in the midst of a starving people. For example, during the fall of 1920 they confiscated for the Red Army two million pounds of potatoes and piled them on the ground at Seelmann and Warenburg on the Meadow Side of the Volga. But the blundering administrators had no means of shipment, and when the frost came the potatoes rotted. They were dumped in the Volga. Resistance by the colonists to such instances of official idiocy were beaten down mercilessly. In March, 1921, some 6,000 starving peasants marched on Communist district headquarters at Balzer. Without warning, the Red Army mowed the protesters down with machine guns.[3]

As the Civil War wound down in the spring of 1921, there was little left in the vast regions most directly affected but starvation, disease, and death. A catastrophic drought now combined with a dearth of seed grain to produce a famine which struck at least 27 million people throughout Russia, and cholera and typhus followed in its train. The Volga colonies produced only 1 percent of their normal grain crop in 1921; it is estimated that 166,000 Germans died of starvation in this region alone. Anna J. Haines, an American relief representative, reported this scene on the Volga:

I could hear the children crying two blocks away as I approached one of the homes for abandoned children in Samara. . . . A steady wail that kept up like a moan grew louder as we got nearer. The nurses could do nothing except to go around every morning and separate the babies that were going to die that day. . . . In the evening those who had died during the day were gathered together and placed in heaps outside the building. A garbage cart stopped each night and the baby bodies were loaded in. . . . In institutions for children under three years of age there is a death rate of 90 percent, and in homes for older children, those from twelve to fifteen years, there is a death rate of 75 percent.[4]

Douglas Hale

Countless thousands died in the Black Sea region as well. Huge areas of Russia had become a charnel house.

Clearly there were adequate grounds to persuade anyone who could escape this hellish existence to consider it seriously. The Mennonites, the best organized of the German colonists, actually succeeded in evacuating some 20,000 of their people to Canada. Most were not so fortunate. Even those Germans who eventually escaped the famine suffered unspeakably in the process. Perhaps a sense of their ordeal may be conveyed by recounting the story of Dave Klein, who began his odyssey from Dreispitz on the Volga to Shattuck, Oklahoma, in December, 1921.

Dave was a cherubic-faced fourteen-year-old when his father, Gottfried Klein, a miller of Dreispitz, at last concluded that his family could no longer endure the murder of their neighbors, the confiscation of their property, the oppression of the authorities, and the specter of starvation. Though he had the cruelest months of the winter before him, he sold what little he owned, stuffed his paper rubles, rendered almost worthless by inflation, into a gunny sack, gathered his family, and fled without even telling his neighbors. Klein planned to join an exodus of 153 Dreispitz refugees fleeing to the west under the pretext of looking for work.

His family consisted of his wife, his elderly mother, a daughter of sixteen, Dave, his eldest son, three younger children, and an infant. They made the first leg of their journey by horse and wagon to Kamyshin, forty miles away, where they joined the larger party. By bribing train crews, the Dreispitz refugees obtained several boxcars for their use. These were partitioned horizontally into two layers, accommodating fifty to sixty people per car. Slowly they made their furtive way to the west, always fearing discovery, repeatedly shunted to sidings and being allowed to continue only after more bribery. Conditions within the cars were appalling; one by one, the weaker members of the group perished. Dave remembered: "First they took Grandma away from us. We were told she died, and were given her clothes, but we don't know what happened. Then the baby got sick, and they took him away from us. . . . He died, and Dad made a coffin for him, and we buried him." The dead were stacked in the cars until their corpses could be disposed of at a safe stopping place.

After about three weeks they arrived at Minsk, only eighteen miles from the Polish border. But there was no shelter for them there, and about fifty members of the party gave up and turned back. They were never heard from again. The leaders of the group had false papers made and hired smugglers to convey the party by sledges to the frontier. Here they were abandoned to their fate. In the dead of night, across the snow-covered fields, Dave and his family crossed into Poland. In the confusion, the children were separated from their parents, and they had to wait an agonizing day before they found each other again.

Poland had been at war with Communist Russia only a few months earlier, but the refugees were permitted to enter. All their money was gone by now, however. The exhausted fugitives walked sixty-three miles to the nearest Polish railway station. The authorities, having no place to put them, loaded them aboard a train to Warsaw. Having appealed for relief in the capital, the refugees were shipped by boxcar to an abandoned military compound at Strzalkowo, about 135 miles west of Warsaw. Here some 600 refugees from all parts of Russia were confined to one dilapidated barracks—cold, wet, miserable, and infested with lice. Dave's father, having risked all in his desperate gamble to escape, became mortally ill and was carried off to the infirmary to die. "Later," Dave remembered, "I went out and I saw they were burning something. It looked like it was all the people that had died—stacked them up and sprayed something on them to make them burn."

At this point, in May, 1922, the Red Cross rescued the survivors. This agency sent a train to Strzalkowo and brought the refugees to the Heimkehr refugee camp near Frankfurt on the Oder, Germany. As the train pulled into the Frankfurt station, the refugees broke into song; their compatriots crowding the platform welcomed them home to Germany with tears. At Heimkehr Camp the Red Cross nursed the people back to life. The attendants shaved their heads, bathed and deloused them, and issued them clothing after their old rags had been burned. Following three weeks of quarantine, the fugitives from the famine were allowed to find work in the area. While Dave and his sister labored in the sugar beet fields near Frankfurt, their mother established contact with Dave's uncles in Oklahoma.

One by one, the survivors of the trek obtained aid from their families and friends abroad. Of the 153 who left Dreispitz, about seventy eventually found their way to America. Sponsored by their kinsmen in Oklahoma, Dave and his family left Germany by way of Bremen and landed in New York on October 22, 1922. A week later they arrived in Shattuck to begin a new life.[5] Though they would be hounded by poverty, depression, and drought as American farmers, their lot would be a far better one than that of their kinsmen who remained behind.

To be sure, the next few years brought a temporary respite in the sufferings of the Germans in Russia. The consequences of the disastrous Civil War, the famine, and the total dislocation of life in the Soviet Union at last persuaded Lenin to adopt a more gradual approach to the communist transformation of the country. This he signaled with the inauguration of the New Economic Policy in 1921. The government made considerable concessions to capitalism, confiscation and requisition of farm production was halted, and the antireligious policy of the Party was somewhat relaxed. About five years thus ensued in which the German colonists were given new hope. They increased their farm production, restored many of their desecrated churches, and began to recoup some of their losses.

But by 1928, Stalin was master of the Soviet Union. He replaced this relatively moderate policy with an all-out drive to collectivize the land of Russia and industrialize it overnight. Millions of lives would be lost in the process. The commissars branded any peasant who had accumulated a few acres of land and some livestock as a "kulak"—marking him out especially as a member of the "rich-farmer" class which was to be liquidated. Many of the German colonists, though poor by any rational definition, fell within this category. The Germans also stubbornly resisted efforts by the regime to take away their land and merge it into collective farms.

Consequently, they suffered horribly in the drive for collectivization between 1928 and 1933. Whole villages were rounded up, herded into railway cars, and shipped to forced labor in the forest camps of the north, to the mines of the Urals, or abandoned to their fate on the steppes of Central Asia. Uprooted from their homes, starved, beaten, and brutalized, tens of thousands perished. Any pretext was sufficient to justify arrest, deportation, and imprisonment. In the town of Seelmann, for instance, a German laborer received a sentence of ten years in a labor camp for filling his pockets with grain while it was being threshed. Usually no pretext was needed. In the Chortitza colony of Franzfeld, for example, of its 630 inhabitants, 85 of the strongest and most productive men and women were arrested and never heard from again. Nearby Burwalde, with a population of 320, lost 72. Blumengart, a village of 273 people, lost 37, and so on.[6]

Estimates range from 400,000 to 100,000 German colonists

interned in the "Gulag Archipelago" during the period of collectivization. Side by side with this program, the Soviet regime intensified its antireligious policy and marked the German clergy for liquidation. In 1914 there had been 198 Lutheran pastors in the German colonies. In 1924, 81 were left. By 1937, there were none.[7] In the Mennonite colonies all religious services were forbidden.

The final blow came in August 1941. Hitler's armies had invaded the Soviet Union the previous June; once again the German colonists were trapped between two hostile armies, forces controlled by the most ruthless tyrannies the century has known. Once again they were made scapegoats for the military failures of the Russian leaders. Branding them as traitors to the motherland, Stalin issued a decree which called for the deportation of all Germans still in European Russia. In every region the Red Army controlled, they herded the helpless victims into cattle cars for transit to the desolate wastes of Siberia or Kazakhstan. Between 650,000 and 700,000 colonists were deported to the east in 1941 and 1942.

With all transportation disrupted by the war, conditions were even worse than before, with the deportees confined to the same car for weeks or even months. One Mennonite from Voronezh commented as follows concerning sanitary facilities:

There was a hole in the corner of our freight car, and everyone: men, women, and children had to use it. We finally lost all feeling of shame. If a baby soiled its diapers, the mother would go to the hole, shake out the diaper and try to wipe it as best she could. She would then put it around her own body, under her skirt, and attempt to dry it in that manner. Wet diapers were handled the same way.[8]

Thousands died in transit, and their bodies were simply dropped beside the tracks. Families were split apart, with the men and childless women assigned to labor camps. The remainder were organized into collective farms under the most primitive conditions. In this way, the Soviet government liquidated the German colonies and scattered their population throughout Asiatic Russia.

Not much better was the fate of the many thousands of refugees who followed the German armies in their retreat westward during the last two years of the war. Thousands were overrun and recaptured by the Red Army; others were interned, deported, or left to swell the destitute mass of displaced persons in postwar Europe.

Until the death of Stalin in 1953, the Germans in Russia simply dropped out of the pages of history: it was as though they had never existed. But belatedly, in the climate of "de-Stalinization" which prevailed after the archtyrant's death, the Soviet regime acknowledged the crimes committed in the process of collectivization. In 1955 interned Germans were released. Nine years later, the Soviet government admitted that the charges of disloyalty against the Russian-Germans which had served as the pretext for their wartime deportation were unfounded. On the contrary, this decree went on, "the overwhelming majority of the German population contributed to the victory of the Soviet Union over fascistic Germany . . . during the great national patriotic war, and have participated actively in the communistic reconstruction in the postwar years." So the Germans were now officially free. Since their former villages had been resettled by Russians, however, the vast majority had no place to go. Only a handful have ventured to return to the remnants of a life they had once known.

According to the most recent census (1970), there were 1,846, 317 Soviet citizens of German ethnic background. Most are widely scattered through Siberia and Central Asia. Today only 4,803 Germans live in the area of the Volga colonies, which had supported half a million before World War I. Forty-six and one-half percent of all the Germans are dispersed throughout the Kazakh Republic, most densely in the Karaganda district. The remainder occupy small ethnic enclaves throughout Siberia or have been thoroughly assimilated into the population among which they were resettled. Before the First World War, only 4.4 percent had lived in cities; today 45.5 percent are urban dwellers. The uniquely German agricultural commonwealth which persisted in Russia for more than a century and a half is no more.[9]

Those who chose the hard road of emigration a century ago chose wisely for themselves and their posterity. They could not have imagined the suffering which fate had in store for their people who remained behind. It required courage to transplant their families from the secure and pleasant villages of Russia to the wild and untilled vastness of the Great Plains and to overcome the enormous obstacles which nature placed in their way. Those who subsequently settled in frontier Oklahoma were no less intrepid in their determination to build a new and abundant life for themselves and their children. Shackled by poverty, living under primitive conditions, wresting a living from a refractory soil, these pioneers found resources of stamina and fortitude which astound those of us accustomed to an easy and comfortable way of life.

If you seek their monument, look around. Though numerically they formed but a small part of Oklahoma's pioneer population, the Germans from Russia have left their stamp upon the land. The most conspicuous landmarks of western Oklahoma are the towering grain elevators whose angular verticality abruptly breaks the broad horizons of the plains. They testify to that generation of farmers who turned the "Great American Desert" into the breadbasket of the world. Among them, the Germans from Russia were in the forefront. The broad expanse of irrigated acres, the neat farmsteads, and the flourishing herds are also part of the legacy of these people.

They contributed also to the essential religiosity of western Oklahoma, which continues to thrive with amazing resilience in the teeth of contemporary materialism. The belief in the inherent virtue of labor—the "work ethic"—that is a powerful force in the region was not only shared but also propagated by these Germans from Russia. The essential conservatism of their way of life is also a part of the western Oklahoma ethos which no stranger can fail to note. Though their children have moved away from the farm, though many occupy positions of influence and prominence in Oklahoma politics, business, education, and industry, the old traditional allegiance to farming, faith, and family, continues to exert its influence on the younger generation.

Today, this posterity looks to the future, not the past. Most of their tenuous ties to the old country were torn asunder during the generation of destruction which overwhelmed their kinsmen in Russia. They are completely and consciously American. Among these people one finds an abiding and profound dedication to American patriotism, not always clearly articulated or fully understood. It is only among the older generation who carry with them memories of the old country and the trials of immigration that the love for America, this new land, reaches its most eloquent and succinct expression. Perhaps Dave Miller, who came to the United States during the Great Famine of 1921, put it best: "Those people who are born in this country don't understand those words that Emma Lazarus wrote that are inscribed in the Statue of Liberty: 'Give me your tired, your poor, your huddled masses yearning to breathe free. . . .' This is something that means the world to us"[10]

Ironically, America closed this "Golden Door" of which Emma Lazarus sang at the very time when the Germans in Russia had most cause to enter it. In 1921 and 1924 the Congress imposed drastic restrictions upon immigration and set rigid quotas which admitted only a small fraction of those who sought access to the United States. In 1913, the last year before World War I, 1,200,000 immigrants had entered this country; Russia alone was sending some 160,000 annually. After the 1924 legislation came into effect, only about 130 immigrants from Russia were admitted each year. With but a few modest exceptions, then, the Russian-German population of the United States received no new influx until after the Second World War when restrictions were somewhat relaxed.

In the meantime, most of the pioneering generation grew old and passed from the scene. A second generation born in America were so caught up in the expansion of the economy during the 1920s or so preoccupied with the harsh realities of the Great Depression that they gave little time or concern to the perpetuation of their unique heritage. Moreover, the regimes which held sway in both Germany and Russia during much of the first half of the twentieth century were so odious in the eyes of most Americans that many of these people were reluctant to identify themselves with either homeland. After all, popular perceptions derived from two world wars and a generalized fear of communism gave the phrase "Russian-German" a somewhat sinister connotation in the public mind. It was difficult for this generation to demonstrate a pride in their heritage or work for its preservation.[11] All the more are we grateful, therefore, for those exceptional individuals who cherished this link with the past in order to transmit it to the future.

For their children, those third-generation Germans from Russia who came to maturity during the 1950s and 1960s, began to seek as though by instinct the ancestral roots from which they sprang. Without shedding an iota of their identity as Americans, they nonetheless were ready to begin the exploration of the past in pursuit of answers to questions which had hardly been framed before: Where did my people come from? How did they fare in this new land? Out of this resurgent interest in the ethnic past, organizations to foster cultural awareness have emerged. A new consciousness of the Russian-German experience has appeared.

BIBLIOGRAPHICAL ESSAY

The most convenient access to materials on this ethnic group is provided through membership in the American Historical Society of Germans from Russia, 631 D Street, Lincoln, Nebraska, 68502, which was founded in 1968. Its quarterly *Journal* contains articles and photographs as well as foreign-language source material appearing in English translation for the first time. The organization serves as a clearing house for genealogical research and makes available books for purchase by the public. This function is particularly important, since owing to their specialized subject matter, works on the Germans from Russia are not ordinarily found in most local bookstores and libraries.

Perhaps the best introduction to the subject is Karl Stumpp, *The German-Russians: Two Centuries of Pioneering* (trans. by J. S. Height, Lincoln, Neb.: American Historical Society of Germans from Russia, 1978), a pictorial survey by the dean of Russian-German historians. More comprehensive is Adam Giesinger's *From Catherine to Khrushchev: The Story of Russia's Germans* (Winnipeg: the author, 1974), which provides both breadth and detail. Fred C. Koch, *The Volga Germans* (University Park, Pa.: Pennsylvania State University Press, 1977), offers an eloquent and informative study of the colonists on Russia's greatest river. In 1973 and 1975 respectively, the North Dakota Historical Society of Germans from Russia, Bismarck, published two books by Joseph S. Height: *Paradise on the Steppe* and *Homesteaders on the Steppe,* which focus upon the settlers of the Ukraine.

As an introduction to the American experience of these people, one should turn to Richard Sallet, *Russian-German Settlements in the United States* (trans. by L. J. Rippley and A. Bauer, Fargo, N. Dak.: North Dakota Institute for Regional Studies, 1974). For the genealogist, two major compendia of immigration lists, village rosters, and parish records are available: Karl Stumpp, *The Emigration from*

Germany to Russia in the Years 1763 to 1862 (Lincoln, Neb.: AHSGR, 1973), and Benjamin H. Unruh, *Die niederländisch-niederdeutschen Hintergründe der mennonitischen Ostwanderungen* (Karlsruhe: Heinrich Scheider, 1955).

Because religion was so central to their lives, the epic of the Russian Germans has often been told in histories of their various faiths. The historically conscious Mennonites have been most successful in keeping their past alive. Dated but still useful is C. Henry Smith, *The Coming of the Russian Mennonites: An Episode in the Settling of the Last Frontier, 1874–1884* (Berne, Ind.: Mennonite Book Concern, 1927). More recently, Harley J. Stucky, *A Century of Russian Mennonite History in America* (North Newton, Kans.: Mennonite Press, 1974), provides a good introduction to the subject, while G. Lorenz, *Heritage Remembered: A Pictorial Survey of Mennonites in Russia and Germany* (Rev. ed., Winnipeg: CMBC Publications, 1977), includes a remarkable collection of photographs. Far more comprehensive than its title suggests, Harold S. Bender and C. Henry Smith, eds., *The Mennonite Encyclopedia* (4 vols., Scottdale, Pa.: Herald Press, 1956–69), is an indispensable reference book for all who are interested in the Germans from Russia.

Published material on other denominations is less readily available, appearing for the most part in periodicals with a regional emphasis and circulation. This holds true as well for studies of the Russian Germans from a local or statewide perspective. For this reason, it is important to have at hand a guide to sources available, which James W. Long, *The German-Russians: A Bibliography* (Santa Barbara: American Bibliographical Center, 1978), provides. The older work by Karl Stumpp, *Das Schrifttum über das Deutschtum in Russland* (2nd ed., Tübingen: the author, 1970), is confined almost exclusively to German-language material which deals with the old-country experience.

As the publication dates of the books listed above suggest, much of what we know about the Germans from Russia has appeared in print very recently indeed. While significant pioneering works are now available, much of the story remains still untold. The letters, memoirs, family and church records, and other documents which will someday help us complete the picture now rest in private hands or archival repositories awaiting the researcher with the time and talent to exploit them. Three of these repositories are particularly important for what they hold relevant to the experience of the Germans from Russia in the Southwest. The Mennonite Library and

Archives, North Newton, Kansas, is richest, of course, in the area of Mennonitica but has abundant materials on other Russian-German denominations as well. The AHSGR Archives and Historical Library, Greeley, Colorado, owns a growing collection of rare books, articles, and documents. Finally, the Colorado Germans from Russia Study Project at Colorado State University, Fort Collins, was founded in 1975 to promote preservation, research, and publication in the field.

For Oklahoma specifically, very little on the Germans from Russia has appeared in print beyond the pioneering works of Vernon R. Wiebe, *Come Let Us Stand United: A History of the Corn Bible Academy, 1902–1977* (Hillsboro, Kans.: the author, 1977), Martha I. Harms, *With Head Held High* (San Antonio: Naylor, 1973), and Lloyd C. Penner, *The Mennonites on the Washita River* (Hillsboro, Kans.: the author, 1976), all of which focus upon Washita County. Two other types of published source materials are quite useful, however: the accounts of individual families which appear in the various Oklahoma county pioneer histories issued recently and the histories of local churches that appear from time to time.

Given the above considerations, it is clear that many fascinating discoveries are yet to be made about the Germans from Russia in Oklahoma. The state of our present knowledge is such that family, church, and local historians can all make significant and revealing contributions to the saga of this people in both the old country and the new. Still living in the small towns of western Oklahoma are men and women who can recall childhood experiences in czarist Russia. Here and there one may find churches and cemeteries which mark the centers of their pioneer community life. Family traditions, customs, recipes, and songs are awaiting the compiler to record them before they are forgotten. Old photographs which speak eloquently of the immigrant experience are gathering dust in neglected attics; packets of old letters remain long forgotten and unread. All these treasures and many more await the explorers of the present who have the time, ingenuity, and patience to unravel the riddles of the past and reconstruct its truth.

NOTES

The following abbreviations are used to designate frequently cited sources or repositories:

AHSGR .... American Historical Society of Germans from Russia, Lincoln, Nebraska
CO   .... *The Chronicles of Oklahoma*
HDR   .... *Heimatbuch der Deutschen aus Russland*
KHQ   .... *Kansas Historical Quarterly*
ME   .... *Mennonite Encyclopedia*
MLA   .... Mennonite Library and Archives, North Newton, Kansas
ML   .... *Mennonite Life*
MQR   .... *Mennonite Quarterly Review*
OSU   .... Oklahoma State University, Stillwater, Oklahoma

CHAPTER 1

1. Map 1, as well as other quantitative data concerning the location and size of the Oklahoma Russian-German communities, is derived from an analysis of the 1910 manuscript census schedules for Oklahoma, United States Bureau of the Census, Personal Service Branch, Pittsburg, Kansas.
2. Except as stipulated otherwise, the account of the German experience in Russia which follows is based upon the following excellent works on the subject: A. Giesinger, *From Catherine to Khrushchev: The Story of Russia's Germans* (Winnipeg: the author, 1974); J. S. Height, *Homesteaders on the Steppe* (Bismarck, N. Dak.: North Dakota Historical Society of Germans from Russia, 1975); F. C. Koch, *The Volga Germans* (University Park, Pa.: Pennsylvania State University Press, 1977); D. G. Rempel, "The Mennonite Commonwealth in Russia: A Sketch of its Founding and Endurance, 1789–1919," *MQR*, XLVII (1973), 259–308, and XLVIII (1974), 5–54; and K. Stumpp, *The German Russians: Two Centuries of Pioneering* (Bonn: Atlantic Forum, 1971).
3. J. A. Duran, Jr., "Catherine II, Potemkin, and Colonization in Southern Russia," *Russian Review*, XXVIII (1969), 23–36.
4. W. Appel, "Versuch einer Festellung der Gründe für die russlanddeutsche Auswanderung aus Hessen," *HDR, 1962,* 59–64.
5. R. Sallet, *Russian-German Settlements in the United States* (Fargo, N. Dak.: North Dakota Institute for Regional Studies, 1974), 23–24, 29, 43–44, 110–111; J. N. Carman, *Foreign Language Units of Kansas* (Lawrence: University of Kansas

The Germans from Russia in Oklahoma

Press, 1962), 132–34, 163–65, 188–95, 260–63; M. E. Johannes, "A Study of the Russian-German Settlements in Ellis County, Kansas," *Catholic University of America Studies in Sociology,* XIV (1946), 1–26; A. Pantle, "Settlement of Krimmer Mennonite Brethren at Gnadenau, Marion County," KHQ, XIII (1945), 259–85. On the question of the introduction of winter wheat, I have followed K. S. Quisenberry and L. P. Reitz, "Turkey Wheat: The Cornerstone of Empire," *Agricultural History,* XLVIII (1974), 98–110. For an opposing view, see N. E. Saul, "The Migration of the Russian-Germans to Kansas," *KHQ,* XL (1974), 38–62.

6. M. Kroeker, "Mennonites in the Oklahoma Runs," *ML,* X (1955), 114; *ME,* III, 652; *Mennonite Weekly Review,* Dec. 26, 1957, 4.

7. Sallet, *Russian-German Settlements,* 12, 20; F. Rink, "The German Settlements in Volhynia," *AHSGR Work Paper,* No. 23 (Spr., 1977), 14–18, and "Wie liegt so weit, was mein einst war: Erinnerungen aus Wolhynien," *HDR, 1962,* 16–26; *ME, IV,* 844–47; H. E. von Wittgenstein, *Mother's Faith—Our Heritage* (Clearbrook, B. C.: the author, n.d.), *passim;* interviews, Lydia Bieberdorf, Stillwater, Okla., July 7, 1974, and July 14, 1978.

8. "Register der deutschen evangelischen Luther Gemeinde bei Orlando und Marina in Payne County, Oklahoma Ty" (MS, Salem Lutheran Church, Stillwater, Okla.); L. Belden, "Salem Evangelical Lutheran Church: A Legacy of Imperial Russia" (Research Paper, OSU, 1971), 11–15; C. L. Petrowsky, ed., *Missouri Synod Lutheranism in Oklahoma, 1890–1974* (Weatherford, Okla.: Weatherford Press, 1974), 2; *Stillwater Daily News Press,* May 6, 1948, 1, 8; interviews, Marie Oltmanns, Stillwater, Okla., July 7, 1974, and February 15, 1979; A. P. DuChateau, "Paul Friedemann, Oklahoma Humanitarian" (MS, Arkansas City, Kan., 1976), 1–10, 16.

9. DuChateau, "Paul Friedemann," *passim;* V. Musick, ed., *Pioneers of Kingfisher County, 1889–1976* (Kingfisher, Okla.: n.p., 1976), 309–11.

CHAPTER 2

1. T. Fontane, *Quitt* (Berlin: W. Herz, 1891).

2. "Autobiography of H. R. Voth," as quoted in J. F. Schmidt, "Heinrich R. Voth (1855–1931)," *MQR,* XL (1966), 217–26; *ME,* I, 48–50, III, 732–37, IV, 858–59, 866–67; Saul, "The Migration of the Russian-Germans to Kansas," 48–51; C. Krehbiel, *Prairie Pioneer* (Newton, Kan.: Faith and Life Press, 1961), 111.

3. On the Darlington Agency, see D. J. Berthrong, *The Cheyenne and Arapaho Ordeal: Reservation and Agency Life in the Indian Territory, 1875–1907* (Norman, Okla.: University of Oklahoma Press, 1976). Voth's missionary activity there is detailed in the following reports incorporated in the *Annual Report of the Commissioner of Indian Affairs to the Secretary of the Interior* for the years indicated: S. S. Haury, *1882,* 62; D. B Dyer, *1884,* 75–77, *1885,* 73–81; and H. R. Voth, *1883,* 68, *1887,* 79–80, *1889,* 310–12, *1890,* 185. See also E. G. Kaufmann, "Mennonite Missions Among the Oklahoma Indians," *CO,* XL (1962), 44–46.

4. See, for example, Voth's articles: "Arapaho Tales," *Journal of American Folklore,* XXV (1912), 43–51, and "Funeral Customs Among the Cheyenne and Arapaho Indians," *Folklorist,* I (1893).

5. Voth, "Historical Notes on the First Decade of the Mennonite Mission Work Among the Hopi of Arizona, 1893–1902," in H. C. James, *Pages from Hopi History* (Tucson: University of Arizona Press, 1974), 153–54. See also Krehbiel, *Prairie*

68

Pioneer, 111, 113–14, 119–20, 124–29; and H. M. Dalke, "Seventy-Five Years of Missions in Oklahoma," *ML,* X (1955), 100–107.

6. F. Waters, *Book of the Hopi* (New York: Viking Press, 1963), 291; interview, Albert Voth, Topeka, Kan., Feb. 1, 1969, by James Juhnke, Showalter Oral History Project, MLA. Voth's major works on the Hopi are published in the *Field Museum of Natural History Anthropological Series,* III, VI, VII, XI (Chicago: Field Museum, 1901–1912).

7. Quoted in H. Courlander, *The Fourth World of the Hopis* (New York: Crown Publishers, 1971), 230. See also Waters, *Book of the Hopi,* 286–97; L. Thompson, *Culture in Crisis: A Study of the Hopi Indians* (New York: Harper and Bros., 1950), 34, fn. 31; P. Qoyawayma, *No Turning Back* (Albuquerque: University of New Mexico Press, 1964), 13–14, 17, 21, 40, 98; and Voth, "Historical Notes," 155–57.

8. V. R. Wiebe, *Come Let Us Stand United: A History of Corn Bible Academy, 1902–1977* (Hillsboro, Kan.: the author, 1977), 5–6; L. C. Penner, "The Mennonites on the Washita River," (Ed.D. diss., OSU, 1976), 110, 121, 171–74; H. H. Flaming, "Reminiscences," in *Wagon Tracks: Washita County Heritage* (Cordell, Okla.: Washita County Historical Committee, 1976), I, 120–21; Krehbiel, *Prairie Pioneer,* 113–16.

9. J. Klaassen, "Memories and Notations About My Life," (trans. by W. Klaassen, MS, n.p., 1966), 2, as quoted in G. Watters, "From Russia to Oklahoma: A Case Study of the Immigrant Experience" (Master's thesis, OSU, 1972), 72.

10. On this episode see F. R. Belk, *The Great Trek of the Russian Mennonites to Central Asia, 1880–1884* (Scottdale, Pa.: Herald Press, 1976), and my own short summary, "From Central Asia to America," *ML,* XXX (1970), 133–38.

11. As quoted in Watters, "From Russia to Oklahoma," 81.

12. Ibid., 82.

13. Belk, *The Great Trek,* 228–29, and "The Final Refuge: Kansas and Nebraska Migration of Mennonites from Central Asia After 1884," *KHQ,* XL (1974), 379–92; Penner, "Mennonites on the Washita River," 188–89; Watters, "From Russia to Oklahoma," 82–90.

14. Oklahoma State Council of Defense, *Sooners in the War* (Oklahoma City, n.p., 1919), 6, as quoted in E. L. Bilger, "The German-Americans in Oklahoma During World War I" (Master's thesis, OSU, 1976), 67. See also O. A. Hilton, "The Oklahoma Council of Defense and the First World War," *CO,* XX (1942), 18–42, and J. H. Fowler, II, "Tar and Feather Patriotism: The Suppression of Dissent in Oklahoma During World War One," *CO,* LVI (1979), 409–30.

15. As quoted in Watters, "From Russia to Oklahoma," 92.

16. Delbert Amen to the author, Oklahoma City, Sept. 11, 1978; Sallet, *Russian-German Settlements,* 47; D. W. Creigh, "The Germans From Russia in Hastings, Nebraska," *AHSGR Work Paper,* No. 17 (Apr., 1975), 38; *Prairie Fire: A Pioneer History of Western Oklahoma* (n.p.: Western Oklahoma Historical Society, 1978), 30-31, 273–74.

17. R. D. Lau to the author, Alva, Okla., Nov. 6, 1978; *Wagon Tracks,* 23, 338, 360–62; A. von Hachenburg, *Ludwig Adolf Peter Fürst zu Sayn und Wittgenstein* (Hannover: Walter Dorn, 1934), 17–25, 181–94.

18. A. J. Becker, "The Story of Post Oak M. B. Mission to the Comanches," *Foreign Missions* (Dec., 1948), 3–16; *ME,* IV, 206; interview, D. C. Peters, Stillwater, Okla., June 19, 1978; C. L. and G. Jackson, *Quanah Parker* (New York: Exposition Press, 1963), 152.

19. J. F. Harms, *Geschichte der Mennoniten Brüdergemeinde* (Hillsboro, Kans.: Mennonite Brethren Publishing House, 1924), 198–99; H. Kloss, *Atlas der in 19. und*

fruhen 20. Jh. entstandenen deutschen Siedlungen in USA (Marburg: N. G. Elwert Verlag, 1974), map L7; J. S. Butler to the author, Stillwater, Okla., Sept. 26, 1978; Kroeker, "Mennonites in the Oklahoma Runs," 119–20; *ME*, II, 551–52.

20. O. Laufer, "The Laufer Journey from the Steppes of the Volga River to the Plains of Oklahoma" (MS, Hobart, Okla., 1970), *passim;* Koch, *The Volga Germans,* 62–63.

CHAPTER 3

1. M. E. Kroeker, "The Mennonites of Oklahoma to 1907," (Master's thesis, University of Oklahoma, 1954), 37–39; *Their Story: A Pioneer Days Album of the Blaine County Area* (Oklahoma City: Heritage Book Committee, 1977), 163–64; "Historical Sketch of the Mennonite Church of Geary, Oklahoma" (n.p., n.d.), *passim; ME*, II, 15–16, 441.

2. Harms, *Geschichte der Mennoniten Brüdergemeinde,* 181–82, 193–98; A. Martens, "History of North M. B. Church," in *Excursions into the Past* (Fairview, Okla.: M. B. Church, 1975), n.p.; E. Sanders, ed., *Blue Skies and Prairie: Okeene Family Histories* (Okeene, Okla.: Okeene Historical Committee, 1977), 44; *Gloss Mountain Country: A History of Major County* (Fairview, Okla.: Major County Historical Society, 1977), I, 391–92.

3. Interview, Peter M. Just, Fairview, Okla., July 31, 1974; Roy Just to the author, Hillsboro, Kans., Nov. 27, 1978; *Gloss Mountain Country,* 184; *ME*, I, 48, III, 132–33.

4. Interviews, Otto Graalman, Okeene, Okla., July 31, 1974, and Harry Haas, Okeene, July 21, 1978; *Kingfisher Free Press: 75th Anniversary Edition,* April 13, 1964, 6, 23; Musick, *Pioneers of Kingfisher County,* 302, 308–10, 354; Sanders, *Blue Skies and Prairie,* 48, 50–51; A. W. Spalding, *Captains of The Host* (Washington, D. C.: Review and Herald Pub. Assoc., 1949), 537–44; M. E. Olson, *A History of the Origin and Progress of Seventh Day Adventists* (Washington, D. C.: Herald Press, 1925), 402–03, 471–81; Sallet, *Russian-German Settlements,* 61; *ME*, I, 141–42, II, 289.

5. Barbara Westfall to the author, Okeene, Okla., Dec. 2, 1978; Sanders, *Blue Skies and Prairie,* 67; J. Schnurr, ed., *Die Kirchen und das religiöse Leben der Russlanddeutschen* [*HDR, 1969–1972*], 119–20; K. Stumpp, *The Emigration from Germany to Russia in the Years 1763 to 1862* (Lincoln, Nebr.: AHSGR, 1973), 81.

6. *Gloss Mountain Country,* 350.

7. Sanders, *Blue Skies and Prairie,* 36, 67, 99–101, 129, 151–55, 218–20; *Their Story, 246.*

8. *Gloss Mountain Country,* 191–92; *Their Story,* 163–64.

9. G. Shirley, *West of Hell's Fringe* (Norman: University of Oklahoma Press, 1978), 205–7, 309, 320; Sanders, *Blue Skies and Prairie,* 122–23, 128.

10. *Gloss Mountain Country,* 30–31; G. Henderson, "Jake Bierig's Story," *Journal of the Cherokee Strip,* X (1968), 24–25; *U. S. District Court Journal,* Woods County Court Records, Reel XLVII, Oklahoma State Archives; *The Alva Pioneer,* Jan. 31, Feb. 21, and May 29, 1896; *The Alva Pioneer-Republican,* Oct. 15, 1897; *AHSGR Clues, 1978,* 59–60; Earl Bierig to the author, Okeene, Okla., Nov. 16, 1978.

11. W. G. Snodgrass, "A History of the Cherokee Outlet" (Ed.D. diss., OSU, 1972), 16–17.

Douglas Hale

12. G. P. Webb, *History of Grant County, Oklahoma, 1811 to 1970* (North Newton, Kans.: Grant County Historical Society, 1971), 148; Kroeker, "The Mennonites of Oklahoma," 66; *ME*, II, 26.

13. Harms, *Geschichte der Mennoniten Brüdergemeinde*, 172–74; *ME*, II, 665, III, 550, IV, 1033–34.

14. Webb, *History of Grant County*, 148; J. Sutherlin, "A History and Analysis of the Churches of Medford, Oklahoma" (MS, Medford Public Library, 1967), 10–11; L. Heller, "The Gaede Ancestral History" (MS, n.p. 1972), *passim; ME*, I, 372, III, 480.

15. S. E. Voth, ed., *Henderson Mennonites: From Holland to Henderson* (Henderson, Neb.: Centennial Committee, 1975), 19–38, 77–81, 125; C. Hiebert, *Hitherto the Lord Has Helped: The Story of the Mennonite Brethren Church North of Enid, Oklahoma, 1897–1957* (Hillsboro, Kans.: Mennonite Brethren Publishing House, 1957), 4–8; Harms, *Geschichte der Mennoniten Brüdergemeinde*, 189–91; *ME*, III, 917; Emanuel Herbert to the author, Breckinridge, Okla., Oct. 24, 1978.

16. Harms, *Geschichte der Mennoniten Brüdergemeinde*, 200–203; *Gloss Mountain Country*, 366, 377–78; *ME*, III, 268, 652, 862, IV, 35–36, 191, 1035.

17. Koch, *The Volga Germans*, 308–9; *Our Alfalfa County Heritage* (Cherokee, Okla.: Alfalfa County Historical Society, 1976), *passim;* Verda McGee to the author, Cherokee, Okla., Jan. 21, 1979; interviews, Mrs. Raymond L. Berry and J. S. Butler, Stillwater, Okla., July 12, 1977; Clarence Beltz, Stillwater, Nov. 28, 1978.

18. Interview, Henry Weber, Cherokee, Okla., Jan. 18, 1975; *Tel-Ectric Topics,* May, 1972, 4; *Our Alfalfa County Heritage,* 437–38.

19. *Pioneer Footprints Across Woods County* (Alva, Okla.: Cherokee Strip Volunteer League, 1976), 88–90, 294, 551–53, 696–98, 751–52; *Sage and Sod: Harper County, Oklahoma, 1885-1973* (2 vols., Buffalo, Okla.: Harper County Historical Society, 1974), I, 222, 464–67, II, 262; R. D. Lau to the author, Alva, Okla., Nov. 6, 1978.

20. *Sage and Sod*, I, 269–70; Godfrey Martin to the author, Buffalo, Okla., Nov. 14, 1978.

21. *Woodward County Pioneer Families* (Woodward, Okla.: Plains Indians and Pioneer Historical Foundation, 1975), 38–39, 133–34, 197–98, 290–91, 373, 378; interview, Mr. and Mrs. Henry G. Hohweiler, Fargo, Okla., July 21, 1978.

22. U. S. Bureau of the Census, *Religious Bodies, 1916* (2 vols., Washington, D. C.: Government Printing Office, 1919), I, 299–300; S. Van Meter, *Marion County Kansas: Past and Present* (Hillsboro, Kan.: Marion County Historical Society, 1972), 209–10; L. Weinbrenner, "The Story of Lehigh" (MS, MLA, 1961), 34–35; D. Baker, ed., *A Pioneer History of Shattuck* (Shattuck, Okla.: n.p., 1970), *passim; Our Ellis County Heritage* (2 vols., Shattuck: Ellis County Historical Society, 1974), I, *passim.*

23. Watters, "From Russia to Oklahoma," 100, 106–14.

24. Baker, *A Pioneer History of Shattuck,* 226–30; Anneva Sander to the author, Seiling, Okla., Jan. 8, 1979; *Ebenezar Baptists in Fifty Years* (Shattuck, Okla.: n.p., 1954), 8.

25. C. C. Rister, *No Man's Land* (Norman: University of Oklahoma Press, 1948), 189; W. L. Shelton, "A History of Texas County, Oklahoma" (Master's thesis, OSU, 1939), 56–58.

26. A. H. Unruh, *Die Geschichte der Mennoniten-Bruedergemeinde* (Hillsboro, Kans.: General Conference of Mennonite Brethren, 1955), 465; Pantle, "Settlement of the Krimmer Mennonite Brethren," 259–85; *ME*, I, 310, 465, II, 136, 530, III, 242–45, IV, 512, 1034–35, 1056.

27. Interviews, Selma Witzke, Alma Lea Hartman, and Mr. and Mrs. Eugene

Martens, Hooker, Okla., and Fred G. Fritzler, Woodward, Okla., July 20, 1978; Mrs. A. L. Lundgrin to the author, Hooker, Jan. 11, 1979.

28. *A History of Beaver County* (2 vols., n.p.: Beaver County Historical Society, 1971), II, 32, 37, 256, 260–61; Unruh, *Geschichte der Mennoniten-Bruedergemeinde*, 185; *50 Anniversary, Bethel Mennonite Brethren Church* (Balko, Okla.: n.p., 1956), 3–8; Mrs. Peggy Goertzen to the author, Balko, Okla., Mar. 16, 1979; *ME*, I, 310, II, 400.

CHAPTER 4

1. D. G. Rempel, "The Expropriation of the German Colonists in South Russia During the Great War," *Journal of Modern History*, IV (1932), 49–67; "Die Verschleppung und Verbannung der Wolhyniendeutschen während des ersten Weltkrieges," *HDR, 1962*, 34–37.

2. F. H. Epp, *Mennonite Exodus* (Altona, Manitoba: D. W. Friesen and Sons, 1962), 36; Giesinger, *From Catherine to Khrushchev*, 264–66.

3. Koch, *The Volga Germans*, 262–63.

4. Quoted in ibid., 266.

5. Interviews, Dave Klein, Wheatridge, Colo., and Dave Miller, Fort Morgan, Colo., Oct. 3, 1965; G. Mueller, "The Trek of 1921–1922" (MS, Tulsa, Okla., 1978), *passim*.

6. J. B. Toews, "Documents on Mennonite Life in Russia, 1930–1940," *AHSGR Work Paper,*No. 19 (Dec., 1975), 11.

7. M. Hagin, "Life in the Volga Colonies From 1921–1941," *AHSGR Work Paper*, No. 12 (Aug., 1973), 7–18; J. S. Height, *Paradise on the Steppe* (Bismarck, N. Dak.: North Dakota Historical Society of Germans from Russia, 1973), 336; Giesinger, *From Catherine to Khrushchev*, 287–92.

8. Quoted in E. S. Haynes, "The Deportation of the Soviet Germans," *AHSGR Work Paper*, No. 24 (Fall, 1977), 11.

9. Koch, *The Volga Germans*, 289–97; Giesinger, *From Catherine to Khrushchev*, 87, 315–35; B. Levytsky, "Germans in the Soviet Union: New Facts and Figures," *AHSGR Work Paper*, No. 22 (Winter, 1976), 2–8.

10. Interview, Dave Miller, Fort Morgan, Colo., Oct. 3, 1965, courtesy of Glenn Mueller, Tulsa.

11. K. W. Rock, *Germans from Russia in America: The First Hundred Years* (Fort Collins, Colo.: Germans from Russia in Colorado Study Project, 1976), 5–6, 8–10.

MAPS

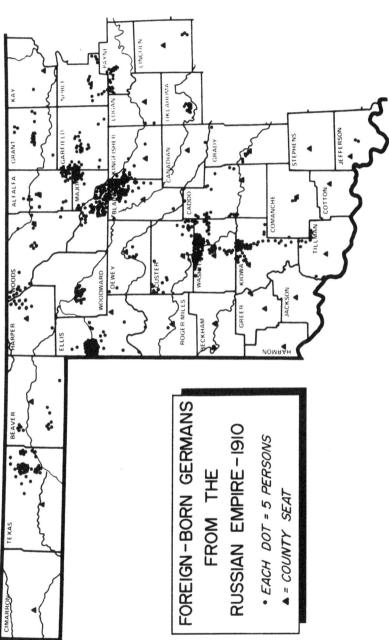

Map 1: Foreign Born Germans from the Russian Empire, 1910

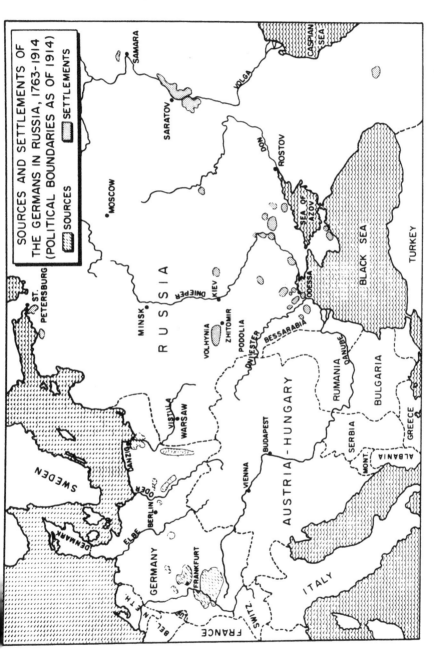

Map 2: Sources and Settlements of the Germans in Russia, 1763–1914

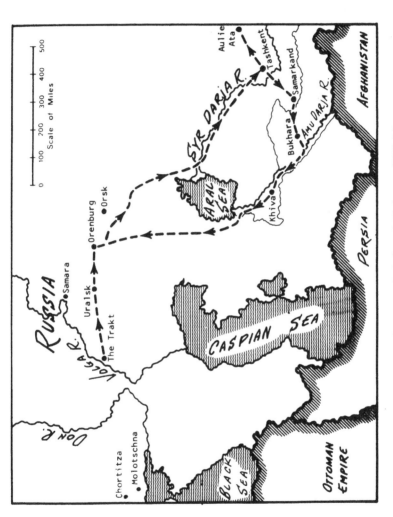

Map 3: The Mennonite Trek through Turkestan, 1880–84

CPSIA information can be obtained
at www.ICGtesting.com
Printed in the USA
BVHW080857141221
624005BV00008B/209

9 780806 116204